Acknowledgments

NIPP 2013: *Partnering for Critical Infrastructure Security and Resilience* was developed through a collaborative process that included the active participation of the critical infrastructure community, including private industry; public and private sector owners and operators; State, local, tribal, and territorial government agencies; non-governmental organizations; Sector-Specific Agencies; and other Federal departments and agencies. This *National Plan* is presented with deepest gratitude, thanks, and appreciation to this diverse community, whose hard work and dedication enabled the development of this document and, most importantly, advance each day the shared mission of strengthening the security and resilience of critical infrastructure.

Table of Contents

List of Figures and Tables

Figures

Tables

Executive Summary

Our national well-being relies upon secure and resilient critical infrastructure—those assets, systems, and networks that underpin American society. To achieve this security and resilience, critical infrastructure partners must collectively identify priorities, articulate clear goals, mitigate risk, measure progress, and adapt based on feedback and the changing environment. *NIPP 2013: Partnering for Critical Infrastructure Security and Resilience* (hereafter referred to as the *National Plan*), guides the national effort to manage risk to the Nation's critical infrastructure.

The community involved in managing risks to critical infrastructure is wide-ranging, composed of partnerships among owners and operators; Federal, State, local, tribal, and territorial governments; regional entities; non-profit organizations; and academia. Managing the risks from significant threat and hazards to physical and cyber critical infrastructure requires an integrated approach across this diverse community to:

- Identify, deter, detect, disrupt, and prepare for threats and hazards to the Nation's critical infrastructure;

- Reduce vulnerabilities of critical assets, systems, and networks; and

- Mitigate the potential consequences to critical infrastructure of incidents or adverse events that do occur.

The success of this integrated approach depends on leveraging the full spectrum of capabilities, expertise, and experience across the critical infrastructure community and associated stakeholders. This requires efficient sharing of actionable and relevant information among partners to build situational awareness and enable effective risk-informed decision making.

In February 2013, the President issued Presidential Policy Directive 21 (PPD-21), *Critical Infrastructure Security and Resilience,* which explicitly calls for an update to the National Infrastructure Protection Plan (NIPP). This update is informed by significant evolution in the critical infrastructure risk, policy, and operating environments, as well as experience gained and lessons learned since the NIPP was last issued in 2009. The *National Plan* builds upon previous NIPPs by emphasizing the complementary goals of security and resilience for critical infrastructure. To achieve these goals, cyber and physical security and the resilience of critical infrastructure assets, systems, and networks are integrated into an enterprise approach to risk management.

The integration of physical and cyber security planning is consistent with Executive Order 13636, *Improving Critical Infrastructure Cybersecurity,* which directs the Federal Government to coordinate with critical infrastructure owners and operators to improve information sharing and collaboratively develop and implement risk-based approaches to cybersecurity. In describing activities to manage risks across the five national preparedness mission areas of prevention, protection, mitigation, response, and recovery, the *National Plan* also aligns with the National Preparedness System called for in Presidential Policy Directive 8 (PPD-8), *National Preparedness.*

Within the context of the risk, policy, and operating environments, critical infrastructure sector and cross-sector partnership structures provide a framework to guide the collective efforts of partners. The national effort to strengthen critical infrastructure security and resilience depends on the ability of public and private critical infrastructure owners and operators to make risk-informed decisions when allocating limited resources in both steady-state and crisis operations.

The value of partnerships under the *National Plan* begins with the direct benefits associated with a clear and shared interest in ensuring the security and resilience of the Nation's critical infrastructure. This baseline value is propagated throughout a network of national, regional, State, and local partnerships between government and owners and operators who have the responsibility of managing risks to enhance security and resilience. For any partnership to be effective, it must provide value to its participants. The value proposition for the government is clear: coordination with infrastructure stakeholders is essential to achieve the government's mandate to preserve public safety and ensure national security. Industry does a great deal to secure its own infrastructure and the welfare of the communities it serves. Government can succeed in encouraging industry to go beyond what is in their commercial interest and invest in the national interest through active engagement in partnership efforts.

For example, the government can provide the private sector with access to timely and actionable information in response to developing threats and crises. In addition, the government can help private sector partners gain a more thorough understanding of the entire risk landscape, enhancing their ability to make informed and efficient security and resilience investments. Finally, industry participants gain an ability to help government planners make better decisions on government security and resilience initiatives, with benefits accruing across critical industry sectors and to the Nation as a whole. As the Nation's critical infrastructure is largely owned by the private sector, managing risk to enhance security and resilience is a shared priority for industry and government.

The *National Plan* establishes a vision, mission, and goals that are supported by a set of core tenets focused on risk management and partnership to influence future critical infrastructure security and resilience planning at the international, national, regional, SLTT, and owner and operator levels. The *National Plan* builds upon the critical infrastructure risk management framework introduced in the 2006 NIPP. Effective risk management requires an understanding of the criticality of assets, systems, and networks, as well as the associated dependencies and interdependencies of critical infrastructure. To this end, the *National Plan* encourages partners to identify critical functions and resources that impact their businesses and communities to support preparedness planning and capability development.

The heart of the *National Plan* is the Call to Action, which guides the collaborative efforts of the critical infrastructure community to advance security and resilience under three broad activity categories: building upon partnership efforts; innovating in managing risk; and focusing on outcomes. The Call to Action provides strategic direction for the national effort in the coming years through coordinated and flexible implementation by Federal departments and agencies—in collaboration with SLTT, regional, and private sector partners, as appropriate. This outcome-driven *National Plan* facilitates the evaluation of progress toward critical infrastructure security and resilience through its goals and priorities and their associated outputs and outcomes.

In conclusion, the *National Plan* describes a national unity of effort to achieve critical infrastructure security and resilience. Given the diverse authorities, roles, and responsibilities of critical infrastructure partners, a proactive and inclusive partnership among all levels of government and the private and non-profit sectors is required to provide optimal critical infrastructure security and resilience. Based on the guidance in the *National Plan*, the partnership will establish and pursue a set of mutual goals and national priorities, and employ common structures and mechanisms that facilitate information sharing and collaborative problem solving.

1. Introduction

Our national well-being relies upon secure and resilient critical infrastructure—those assets, systems and networks that underpin American society. The purpose of the NIPP 2013: *Partnering for Critical Infrastructure Security and Resilience* (hereafter referred to as the *National Plan*), is to guide the national effort to manage risks to the Nation's critical infrastructure. To achieve this end, critical infrastructure partners must collectively identify national priorities; articulate clear goals; mitigate risk; measure progress; and adapt based on feedback and the changing environment. Success in this complex endeavor leverages the full spectrum of capabilities, expertise, and experience from across a robust partnership.

This *National Plan* builds on and supersedes the 2009 *National Infrastructure Protection Plan* and recognizes the valuable progress made to date to protect the Nation's critical infrastructure. It reflects changes in the critical infrastructure risk, policy, and operating environments and is informed by the need to integrate the cyber, physical, and human elements of critical infrastructure in managing risk. The *National Plan* guides national efforts, drives progress, and engages the broader community about the importance of critical infrastructure security and resilience.

The audience for this plan includes a wide-ranging critical infrastructure community comprised of public and private critical infrastructure owners and operators; Federal departments and agencies, including Sector-Specific Agencies (SSAs); State, local, tribal, and territorial (SLTT) governments; regional entities; and other private and non-profit organizations charged with securing and strengthening the resilience of critical infrastructure.

Managing risks to critical infrastructure requires an integrated approach across this broad community to:

- Identify, deter, detect, disrupt, and prepare for threats and hazards to the Nation's critical infrastructure;

- Reduce vulnerabilities of critical assets, systems, and networks; and

- Mitigate the potential consequences to critical infrastructure of incidents or adverse events that do occur.

Given the diverse authorities, roles, and responsibilities of critical infrastructure partners, flexible, proactive, and inclusive partnerships are required to advance critical infrastructure security and resilience. Presidential Policy Directive 21 (PPD-21) notes, "Critical infrastructure owners and operators are uniquely positioned to manage risks to their individual operations and assets, and to determine effective strategies to make them more secure and resilient." Individual efforts to manage risk are enhanced by a collaborative public-private partnership that operates as a unified national effort, as opposed to a hierarchical, command-and-control structure. PPD-21 stresses the distributed nature of critical infrastructure as well as the varied authorities and responsibilities of partners by noting that critical infrastructure includes "distributed networks, varied organizational structures and operating models (including multinational and international ownership), interdependent functions and systems in both the physical space and cyberspace, and governance constructs that involve multi-level authorities, responsibilities, and regulations."[1] The *National Plan* recognizes that public-private collaboration is built on a trusted environment, where processes for information sharing improve situational awareness, and remain open and transparent while protecting privacy and civil liberties.

The *National Plan* takes into account the varying risk management perspectives of the public and private sectors, where government and private industry have aligned, but not identical, interests in securing critical infrastructure and making it more resilient. It leverages comparative advantages of both the private and public sectors to the mutual benefit of all. The *National Plan* is organized in the following manner:

---

[1] The White House, Presidential Policy Directive 21 – Critical Infrastructure Security and Resilience, http://www.whitehouse.gov/the-press-office/2013/02/12/presidential-policy-directive-critical-infrastructure-security-and-resil, accessed September 24, 2013.

- **Section 2 – Vision, Mission, and Goals** – Outlines the vision, mission, and goals for the critical infrastructure community.

- **Section 3 – Critical Infrastructure Environment** – Describes the policy, risk, and operating environments, as well as the partnership structure within which the community undertakes efforts to achieve goals aimed at strengthening security and resilience.

- **Section 4 – Core Tenets** – Describes the principles and assumptions that underpin this *National Plan*.

- **Section 5 – Collaborating to Manage Risk** – Describes a common framework for risk management activities conducted by the critical infrastructure community in the context of national preparedness.

- **Section 6 – Call to Action** – Calls upon the critical infrastructure community (respective of authorities, responsibilities, and business environments) to take cross-cutting, proactive, and coordinated actions that support collective efforts to strengthen critical infrastructure security and resilience in the coming years.

- **Glossary of Terms**

- **Appendices**

Several supplemental resources will be offered to provide guidance and assistance to the critical infrastructure community as part of implementing the *National Plan*. These supplements will be stand-alone resources and will include, among other topics, executing a critical infrastructure risk management approach; connecting to the National Cybersecurity and Communications Integration Center (NCCIC) and the National Infrastructure Coordinating Center (NICC); resources for vulnerability assessments; and incorporating resilience into critical infrastructure projects. These will be available online and regularly updated for easy access by the critical infrastructure community.

Evolution From the 2009 NIPP

The *National Plan* continues to focus on risk management as the foundation of critical infrastructure security and resilience and promotes partnerships as the key mechanism through which risks are managed. In doing so, it reaffirms the role of various coordinating structures including Sector Coordinating Councils, Government Coordinating Councils, and cross-sector councils. Building on progress made toward critical infrastructure security and resilience by those councils and others over the past 10 years, this *National Plan*:

- Elevates security and resilience as the primary aim of critical infrastructure homeland security planning efforts;

- Updates the critical infrastructure risk management framework and addresses alignment to the National Preparedness System, across the prevention, protection, mitigation, response, and recovery mission areas;

- Focuses on establishing a process to set critical infrastructure national priorities determined jointly by the public and private sector;

- Integrates cyber and physical security and resilience efforts into an enterprise approach to risk management;

- Affirms that critical infrastructure security and resilience efforts require international collaboration;

- Supports execution of the *National Plan* and achievement of the National Preparedness Goal at both the national and community levels, with focus on leveraging regional collaborative efforts; and

- Presents a detailed Call to Action with steps that will be undertaken, shaped by each sector's priorities and in collaboration with critical infrastructure partners, to make progress toward security and resilience.

2. Vision, Mission, and Goals

The strategic direction for efforts to build and sustain critical infrastructure security and resilience is driven by a common vision and mission.

Vision

A Nation in which physical and cyber critical infrastructure remain secure and resilient, with vulnerabilities reduced, consequences minimized, threats identified and disrupted, and response and recovery hastened.

Mission

Strengthen the security and resilience of the Nation's critical infrastructure, by managing physical and cyber risks through the collaborative and integrated efforts of the critical infrastructure community.

The vision and mission depend on the achievement of goals that represent the strategic direction on which critical infrastructure activities should be focused over the next several years.

Goals

- Assess and analyze threats to, vulnerabilities of, and consequences to critical infrastructure to inform risk management activities;
- Secure critical infrastructure against human, physical, and cyber threats through sustainable efforts to reduce risk, while accounting for the costs and benefits of security investments;
- Enhance critical infrastructure resilience by minimizing the adverse consequences of incidents through advance planning and mitigation efforts, and employing effective responses to save lives and ensure the rapid recovery of essential services;
- Share actionable and relevant information across the critical infrastructure community to build awareness and enable risk-informed decision making; and
- Promote learning and adaptation during and after exercises and incidents.

These goals will be augmented by the regular development of more specific priorities by the critical infrastructure partnership related to risk management and capability enhancement.

Based on the vision, mission, and goals, the critical infrastructure community will work jointly to set specific national priorities, while considering resource availability, progress already made, known capability gaps, and emerging risks. These priorities should drive action nationally and will be supplemented by sector, regional, and SLTT priorities. Performance measures will be set based on the goals and priorities. The National Annual Report and the National Preparedness Report include measurements of progress, which will help build a common understanding of the state of critical infrastructure security and resilience efforts. The interrelationship of these elements is depicted in Figure 1.

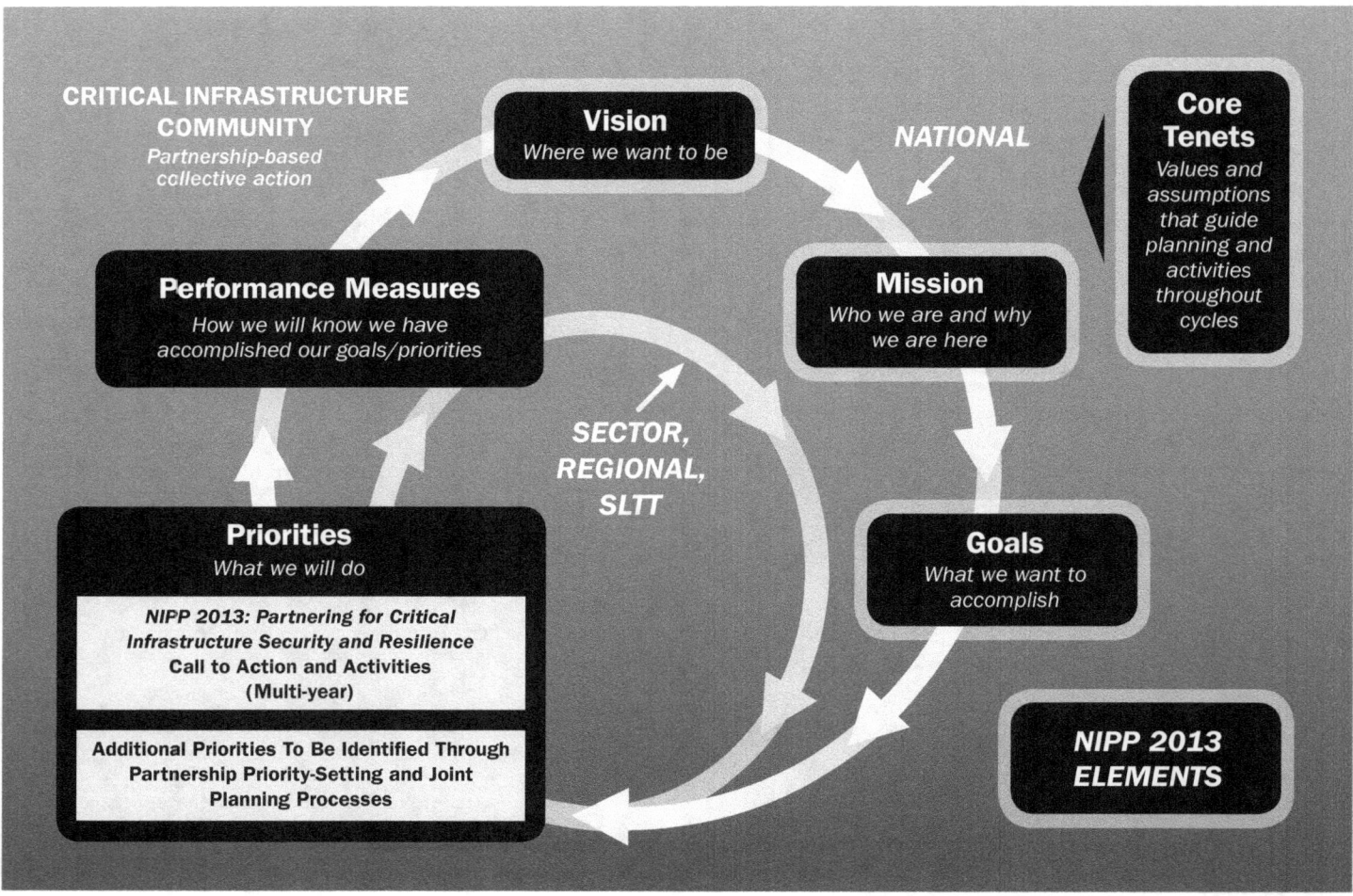

3. Critical Infrastructure Environment

This *National Plan* relies on several key concepts, which remain consistent with the 2009 NIPP. At the same time, the Plan is informed by and updated to reflect the evolving critical infrastructure risk, policy, and operating environments. This section describes the changes in the critical infrastructure environment since the publication of the last NIPP, while affirming the importance of successful collaboration across the core partnership structure to manage risks.

Key Concepts

The key concepts described below provide context for this critical infrastructure environment. An understanding of these key concepts influences the state of critical infrastructure and shapes the community's approach to ensuring security and resilience.

- **Critical infrastructure** represents "systems and assets, whether physical or virtual, so vital to the United States that the incapacity or destruction of such systems and assets would have a debilitating impact on security, national economic security, national public health or safety, or any combination of those matters."[2] The *National Plan* acknowledges that the Nation's critical infrastructure is largely owned and operated by the private sector; however, Federal and SLTT governments also own and operate critical infrastructure, as do foreign entities and companies.

- PPD-21 defines **security** as "reducing the risk to critical infrastructure by physical means or defens[ive] cyber measures to intrusions, attacks, or the effects of natural or manmade disasters." There are several elements of securing critical infrastructure systems, including addressing threats and vulnerabilities and sharing accurate information and analysis on current and future risks. Prevention and protection activities contribute to strengthening critical infrastructure security.

- **Resilience**, as defined in PPD-21, is "the ability to prepare for and adapt to changing conditions and withstand and recover rapidly from disruptions...[it] includes the ability to withstand and recover from deliberate attacks, accidents, or naturally occurring threats or incidents." Having accurate information and analysis about risk is essential to achieving resilience. Resilient infrastructure assets, systems, and networks must also be robust, agile, and adaptable. Mitigation, response, and recovery activities contribute to strengthening critical infrastructure resilience.

- Security and resilience are strengthened through risk management. **Risk** refers to the "potential for an unwanted outcome resulting from an incident, event, or occurrence, as determined by its likelihood [a function of threats and vulnerabilities] and the associated consequences;" **risk management** is the "process of identifying, analyzing, and communicating risk and accepting, avoiding, transferring, or controlling it to an acceptable level at an acceptable cost."[3]

- **Partnerships** enable more effective and efficient risk management. Within the context of this *National Plan*, a partnership is defined as close cooperation between parties having common interests in achieving a shared vision. For the critical infrastructure community, leadership involvement, open communication, and trusted relationships are essential elements to partnership.

---

[2] USA Patriot Act of 2001 § 1016(e).
[3] U.S. Department of Homeland Security, DHS Risk Lexicon – 2010 Edition, September 2010, http://www.dhs.gov/xlibrary/assets/dhs-risk-lexicon-2010.pdf

Risk Environment

The risk environment affecting critical infrastructure is complex and uncertain; threats, vulnerabilities, and consequences have all evolved over the last 10 years. For example, critical infrastructure that has long been subject to risks associated with physical threats and natural disasters is now increasingly exposed to cyber risks, which stems from growing integration of information and communications technologies with critical infrastructure operations and an adversary focus on exploiting potential cyber vulnerabilities. Figure 2 illustrates the evolving threats to critical infrastructure.

The Strategic National Risk Assessment[4] (SNRA) defines numerous threats and hazards to homeland security in the broad categories of adversarial/human-caused, natural, and technological/accidental threats. Critical assets, systems, and networks face many of the threats categorized by the SNRA, including terrorists and other actors seeking to cause harm and disrupt essential services through physical and cyber attacks, severe weather events, pandemic influenza or other health crises, and the potential for accidents and failures due to infrastructure operating beyond its intended lifespan. The potential for interconnected events with unknown consequences adds uncertainty in addition to the known risks analyzed as part of the SNRA.

Growing interdependencies across critical infrastructure systems, particularly reliance on information and communications technologies, have increased the potential vulnerabilities to physical and cyber threats and potential consequences resulting from the compromise of underlying systems or networks. In an increasingly interconnected world, where critical infrastructure crosses national borders and global supply chains, the potential impacts increase with these interdependencies and the ability of a diverse set of threats to exploit them.

Figure 2 – Evolving Threats to Critical Infrastructure

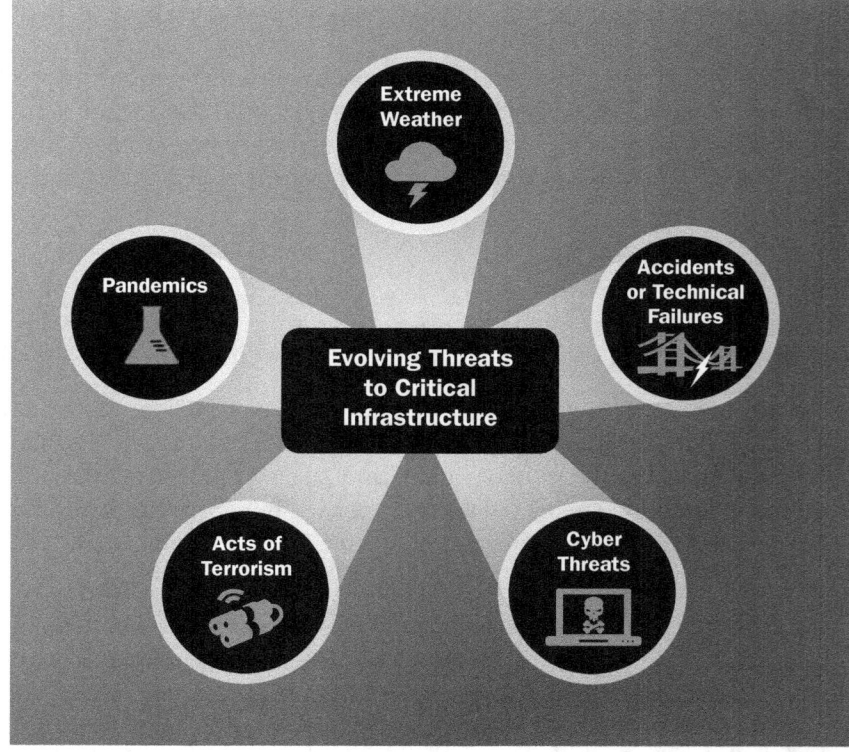

In addition, the effects of extreme weather pose a significant risk to critical infrastructure—rising sea levels, more severe storms, extreme and prolonged drought conditions, and severe flooding combine to threaten infrastructure that provides essential services to the American public. Ongoing and future changes to the climate[5] have the potential to compound these risks and could have a major impact on infrastructure operations.

Finally, vulnerabilities also may exist as a result of a retiring work force or lack of skilled labor. Skilled operators are necessary for infrastructure maintenance and, therefore, security and resilience. These various factors influence the risk environment and, along with the policy and operating environments, create the backdrop against which decisions are made for critical infrastructure security and resilience.

Policy Environment

Title II of the Homeland Security Act of 2002 (as amended) details the Department of Homeland Security's (DHS) responsibilities for critical infrastructure security and resilience. Under the act, DHS must develop a comprehensive plan for securing the

---

[4] U.S. Department of Homeland Security, Strategic National Risk Assessment, December 2011, http://www.dhs.gov/xlibrary/assets/rma-strategic-national-risk-assessment-ppd8.pdf
[5] The National Security Strategy states that "the danger from climate change is real, urgent, and severe." National Security Strategy, 2010.

Nation's critical infrastructure. DHS completed the first version of the NIPP in 2006, and issued an update in 2009. Since 2009, numerous national policies have continued to shape the way the Nation addresses critical infrastructure security and resilience and national preparedness.

On February 12, 2013, the President issued PPD-21, *Critical Infrastructure Security and Resilience*, which explicitly calls for the development of an updated national plan. The directive builds on the extensive work done to date to protect critical infrastructure, and describes a national effort to share threat information, reduce vulnerabilities, minimize consequences, and hasten response and recovery efforts related to critical infrastructure. It also identifies 16 critical infrastructure sectors, listed in the box on the right.[6]

The President also issued Executive Order 13636: *Improving Critical Infrastructure Cybersecurity* in February of 2013, which calls for the Federal Government to closely coordinate with critical infrastructure owners and operators to improve cybersecurity information sharing and collaboratively develop and implement risk-based approaches to cybersecurity.[7] The executive order directs the Federal Government to develop a technology-neutral cybersecurity framework to reduce cyber risk to critical infrastructure; promote and incentivize the adoption of strong cybersecurity practices; increase the volume, timeliness, and quality of information sharing related to cyber threats; and incorporate protection for privacy and civil liberties into critical infrastructure security and resilience initiatives.

• Chemical	• Food and Agriculture
• Commercial Facilities	• Government Facilities
• Communications	• Healthcare and Public Health
• Critical Manufacturing	
• Dams	• Information Technology
• Defense Industrial Base	• Nuclear Reactors, Materials, and Waste
• Emergency Services	• Transportation Systems
• Energy	• Water and Wastewater Systems
• Financial Services	

The *National Plan* is aligned with the goal of PPD-8, *National Preparedness*, of "a secure and resilient Nation with the capabilities required across the whole community to prevent, protect against, mitigate, respond to, and recover from the threats and hazards that pose the greatest risk." These five PPD-8 mission areas are central to a comprehensive approach for enhancing national preparedness and critical infrastructure risk management activities across all five mission areas contribute to achieving the National Preparedness Goal. In addition, the *National Plan* is consistent with the National Planning Frameworks and Interagency Operational Plans developed pursuant to PPD-8. The scope of the *National Plan* is not meant to and does not alter the implementation and execution of prevention activities, as described in the Prevention Federal Interagency Operational Plan. The *National Plan* scope comprises activities that often support and abut prevention activities designed to avoid, prevent, or stop an imminent threat or actual attacks.

Two additional policy documents that align with this *National Plan* include the President's *Climate Action Plan*, issued in June 2013, and the *National Strategy for Information Sharing and Safeguarding* (NSISS), issued in December 2013. The *Climate Action Plan* establishes a number of strategic objectives and directs Federal agencies to take further action to better prepare America for the impacts of climate change, including enhancing the resilience of infrastructure. The NSISS identifies as one of 16 national priorities the need to establish "information-sharing processes and sector-specific protocols with private sector partners, to improve information quality and timeliness and secure the Nation's infrastructure."

Operating Environment

The extent to which infrastructure is interconnected shapes the environment for critical infrastructure security and resilience by necessitating collaboration in both planning and action. The Nation's critical infrastructure has become much more interdependent, continuing to move from an operating environment characterized by disparate assets, systems, and networks to one in which cloud computing, mobile devices, and wireless connectivity have dramatically changed the way infrastructure is operated. Interdependencies may be operational (e.g., power required to operate a water pumping station) or physical (e.g., co-located infrastructure, such as water and electric lines running under a bridge span). Interdependencies may be limited to small urban or rural areas or span vast regions, crossing jurisdictional and national boundaries, including infrastructure that require accurate and precise positioning, navigation, and timing (PNT) data. PNT services are critical to the operations of multiple critical infrastructure sectors and are vital to incident response.

---

[6] The White House, Presidential Policy Directive 21 — Critical Infrastructure Security and Resilience, http://www.whitehouse.gov/the-press-office/2013/02/12/presidential-policy-directive-critical-infrastructure-security-and-resil, accessed Aug. 6, 2013.
[7] The White House, Executive Order 13636 — Improving Critical Infrastructure Cybersecurity, http://www.gpo.gov/fdsys/pkg/FR-2013-02-19/pdf/2013-03915.pdf, accessed Aug. 22, 2013

The Nation has benefited from the investments made in increased security and resilience by both public and private sector owners and operators. Much of the critical infrastructure community continues to integrate cybersecurity into core business practices, making significant investments to increase security and resilience. In other areas, however, despite public and private sector expenditures to operate and maintain critical infrastructure systems, the level of investment has not been adequate, as evidenced by the deteriorating condition of many infrastructure systems. The National Academy of Sciences reported that the Nation's earlier heavy investment in the design, construction, and operation of critical infrastructure systems—water, wastewater, energy, transportation, and telecommunications—has not been matched with the funds necessary to keep these systems in good condition or to upgrade them to meet the demands of a growing and shifting population.[8]

Critical infrastructure assets, systems, and networks, as well as other key resources, reside in particular jurisdictions, but their resulting information, products, services, and functions can be provided worldwide. The nature of critical infrastructure ownership and operations is also distributed, and the need for joint planning and investment is becoming more common and necessary on the international level. These global connections inform the way that the critical infrastructure community should plan to work together, within and across sectors, and across jurisdictions and national borders, to increase the security and resilience of critical infrastructure. Information security and privacy considerations also shape the operating environment. The increasing availability of data and information essential to operating and maintaining infrastructure and related technologies enables more efficient and effective practices. This information is vulnerable to unauthorized access that could affect its confidentiality, integrity, or availability. The distribution of such information to those entities that can use it for efficient and effective risk management remains a challenge. It is critical to maintain the availability of information and distribute it to those who can use and protect it properly. This entails being transparent about information-sharing practices; protecting sources and methods; and ensuring privacy[9] and protecting civil liberties, while also enabling law enforcement investigations.

This complex environment underscores the challenge in securing and strengthening the resilience of the Nation's critical infrastructure. Because of the dynamic nature of this environment, the ability to consistently partner to take advantage of unique skills and capabilities across the community remains the foundation for critical infrastructure security and resilience efforts.

Partnership Structure

Voluntary collaboration between private sector owners and operators (including their partner associations, vendors, and others) and their government counterparts has been and will remain the primary mechanism for advancing collective action toward national critical infrastructure security and resilience. The Federal Government must make economic calculations of risk while also considering many non-economic values, such as privacy concerns, when addressing its role in national and homeland security. As a result, government may have a lower tolerance for security risk than a commercial entity. Both perspectives are legitimate, but in a world in which reliance on critical infrastructure is shared by industry and government and where industry may be on the front lines of national defense, such as in a cyber attack, a sustainable partnership must be developed to address both perspectives.

As the nature of the critical infrastructure risk environment precludes any one entity from managing risks entirely on its own, partners benefit from access to knowledge and capabilities that would otherwise be unavailable to them. Many critical infrastructure sectors have worked to establish stable and representative partnerships, managing transitions in leadership and broadening the range of members and skill sets needed to accomplish collective goals. In addition, through trusted relationships and information sharing, Federal agencies gain a better understanding of the risks and preparedness posture associated with critical infrastructure. This allows entities to make more informed decisions when identifying and addressing national critical infrastructure priorities. Participation in this effort is based on a clear and shared interest in ensuring the security and resilience of the Nation's critical infrastructure and an understanding of the comparative advantage each element of the partnership can bring to achieve this shared interest.

The *National Plan* organizes critical infrastructure into 16 sectors and designates a Federal department or agency as the lead coordinator—Sector-Specific Agency (SSA)—for each sector (refer to Appendix B for the roles and responsibilities of SSAs). The sector and cross-sector partnership council structures described in previous NIPPs remain the foundation for this *National Plan* and are depicted in Table 1.

---

[8] National Academy of Sciences, National Research Council, Sustainable Critical Infrastructure Systems, A Framework for Meeting 21st Century Imperatives, 2009.
[9] Applying Fair Information Practice Principles (FIPPs) to government and private sector stakeholder programs is a best practice for ensuring that privacy protections are included. The FIPPs are the widely-accepted framework of principles used to assess and mitigate privacy impacts of information systems, processes, or programs. The FIPPs are eight interdependent principles: Transparency, Individual Participation, Purpose Specification, Data Minimization, Use Limitation, Data Quality and Integrity, Security, and Accountability and Auditing. These principles form a framework that can be applied to any type of information collection, use, or sharing activity; the exact implementation of each principle, however, will vary based upon context.

Table 1 – Sector and Cross-Sector Coordinating Structures

| Critical Infrastructure Sector | Sector-Specific Agency | Critical Infrastructure Partnership Advisory Council | | |
		Sector Coordinating Councils (SCCs)	Government Coordinating Councils (GCCs)	Regional Consortia
Chemical	Department of Homeland Security	✓	✓	
Commercial Facilities ⓘ		✓	✓	
Communications ⓘ		✓	✓	
Critical Manufacturing		✓	✓	
Dams		✓	✓	
Emergency Services ⓘ		✓	✓	
Information Technology ⓘ		✓	✓	
Nuclear Reactors, Materials & Waste		✓	✓	
Food & Agriculture	Department of Agriculture, Department of Health and Human Services	✓	✓	
Defense Industrial Base ⓘ	Department of Defense	✓	✓	
Energy ⓘ	Department of Energy	✓	✓	
Healthcare & Public Health ⓘ	Department of Health and Human Services	✓	✓	
Financial Services ⓘ	Department of the Treasury	Uses separate coordinating entity	✓	
Water & Wastewater Systems ⓘ	Environmental Protection Agency	✓	✓	
Government Facilities	Department of Homeland Security, General Services Administration	Sector does not have an SCC	✓	
Transportation Systems ⓘ	Department of Homeland Security, Department of Transportation	Various SCCs are broken down by transportation mode or subsector.	✓	

Arrows spanning the council columns are labeled:
- Critical Infrastructure Cross-Sector Council (SCCs)
- Federal Senior Leadership Council (GCCs)
- State, Local, Tribal, and Territorial Government Coordinating Council
- Regional Consortium Coordinating Council

ⓘ Indicates that a sector (or a subsector within the sector) has a designated information-sharing organization.

Sector and cross-sector council structures include:

- **Sector Coordinating Councils (SCCs)** – Self-organized, self-run, and self-governed private sector councils consisting of owners and operators and their representatives, which interact on a wide range of sector-specific strategies, policies, activities, and issues. SCCs serve as principal collaboration points between the government and private sector owners and operators for critical infrastructure security and resilience policy coordination and planning and a range of related sector-specific activities.

- **Critical Infrastructure Cross-Sector Council** – Consisting of the chairs and vice chairs of the SCCs, this private sector council coordinates cross-sector issues, initiatives, and interdependencies to support critical infrastructure security and resilience.

- **Government Coordinating Councils (GCCs)** – Consisting of representatives from across various levels of government (including Federal and SLTT), as appropriate to the operating landscape of each individual sector, these councils enable interagency, intergovernmental, and cross-jurisdictional coordination within and across sectors and partner with SCCs on public-private efforts.

- **Federal Senior Leadership Council (FSLC)** – Consisting of senior officials from the SSAs and other Federal departments and agencies with a role in critical infrastructure security and resilience, the FSLC facilitates communication and coordination on critical infrastructure security and resilience across the Federal Government.

- **State, Local, Tribal, and Territorial Government Coordinating Council (SLTTGCC)** – Consisting of representatives from across SLTT government entities, the SLTTGCC promotes the engagement of SLTT partners in national critical infrastructure security and resilience efforts and provides an organizational structure to coordinate across jurisdictions on State and local government guidance, strategies, and programs.

- **Regional Consortium Coordinating Council (RC3)** – Comprises regional groups and coalitions around the country engaged in various initiatives to advance critical infrastructure security and resilience in the public and private sectors.

- **Information Sharing Organizations** – Organizations including Information Sharing and Analysis Centers (ISACs) serve operational and dissemination functions for many sectors, subsectors, and other groups, and facilitate sharing of information between government and the private sector. ISACs also collaborate on a cross-sector basis through a national council.

Note: Appendix A further describes the functions of the above partnership structures, as well as additional structures that support national critical infrastructure security and resilience.

The sector and cross-sector partnership approach described above is designed to be scalable and allow individual owners and operators of critical infrastructure and other stakeholders across the country to participate. It is intended to promote consistency of process to enable efficient collaboration between disparate parts of the critical infrastructure community, while allowing for the use of other viable partnership structures and planning processes. This concept has proved successful and can be leveraged at the State, local, tribal, and territorial levels as well as within and across regions to build, form, or expand existing networks; identify proven practices; adapt to or adopt lessons learned; and leverage practices, processes, or plans as appropriate.

Many of the listed structures take advantage of the Critical Infrastructure Partnership Advisory Council (CIPAC).[10] The Secretary of Homeland Security established CIPAC in 2006 as a mechanism to directly support sectors' interest to engage in public-private critical infrastructure discussions and participate in a broad spectrum of activities. CIPAC exempts partnership meetings from the Federal Advisory Committee Act (FACA), allowing the public-private critical infrastructure community to engage in frank or sensitive dialogue to mitigate critical infrastructure vulnerabilities and lessen impacts from developing or emerging threats.[11] Specifically, CIPAC forums support Federal Government deliberations on critical infrastructure issues that are needed to arrive at a consensus position or when making formal recommendations. CIPAC also may be used at the sector, cross-sector, or working group level, depending on the topic and deliberation purpose. Other Federal agencies also may have and utilize FACA-exempt committees and advisory councils to engage with the private sector; however, the CIPAC model provides the legal framework for cross-sector collaboration.

---

[10] Critical Infrastructure Partnership Advisory Council, http://www.dhs.gov/critical-infrastructure-partnership-advisory-council
[11] Federal Advisory Committee Act, Public Law 92–463 (October 6, 1972).

4. Core Tenets

The *National Plan* establishes seven core tenets, representing the values and assumptions the critical infrastructure community should consider (at the national, regional, SLTT, and owner and operator levels) when planning for critical infrastructure security and resilience.

1. **Risk should be identified and managed in a coordinated and comprehensive way across the critical infrastructure community to enable the effective allocation of security and resilience resources.**

   Collaboratively managing risk requires sharing information (including smart practices), promoting more efficient and effective use of resources, and minimizing duplication of effort. It enables the development and execution of more comprehensive measures to secure against, disrupt, and prepare for threats; mitigate vulnerabilities; and reduce consequences across the Nation. To ensure a comprehensive approach to risk management, the critical infrastructure community considers strategies to achieve risk mitigation, as well as other ways to address risk, including acceptance, avoidance, or transference.

2. **Understanding and addressing risks from cross-sector dependencies and interdependencies is essential to enhancing critical infrastructure security and resilience.**

   The way infrastructure sectors interact, including through reliance on shared information and communications technologies (e.g., cloud services), shapes how the Nation's critical infrastructure partners should collectively manage risk. For example, all critical infrastructure sectors rely on functions provided by energy, communications, transportation, and water systems, among others. In addition, interdependencies flow both ways, as with the dependence of energy and communications systems on each other and on other functions. It is important for the critical infrastructure community to understand and appropriately account for dependencies and interdependencies when managing risk.

3. **Gaining knowledge of infrastructure risk and interdependencies requires information sharing across the critical infrastructure community.**

   Through their operations and perspectives, stakeholders across the critical infrastructure community possess and produce diverse information useful to the enhancement of critical infrastructure security and resilience. Sharing and jointly planning based on this information is imperative to comprehensively address critical infrastructure security and resilience in an environment of increasing interconnectedness. For that to happen, appropriate legal protections, trusted relationships, enabling technologies, and consistent processes must be in place.

4. **The partnership approach to critical infrastructure security and resilience recognizes the unique perspectives and comparative advantages of the diverse critical infrastructure community.**

   The public-private partnership is central to maintaining critical infrastructure security and resilience. A well-functioning partnership depends on a set of attributes, including trust; a defined purpose for its activities; clearly articulated goals; measurable progress and outcomes to guide shared activities; leadership involvement; clear and frequent communication; and flexibility and adaptability. All levels of government and the private and nonprofit sectors bring unique expertise, capabilities, and core competencies to the national effort. Recognizing the value of different perspectives helps the partnership more distinctly understand challenges and solutions related to critical infrastructure security and resilience.

5. **Regional and SLTT partnerships are crucial to developing shared perspectives on gaps and actions to improve critical infrastructure security and resilience.**

   The *National Plan* emphasizes partnering across institutions and geographic boundaries to achieve security and resilience. Risks often have local consequences, making it essential to execute initiatives on a regional scale in a way that complements and operationalizes the national effort. This requires locally based public, private, and non-profit organizations to provide their perspectives in the assessment of risk and mitigation strategies. Local partnerships throughout the country augment the efforts of existing partnerships at the national level and are essential to a true national effort to strengthen security and resilience.

6. **Infrastructure critical to the United States transcends national boundaries, requiring cross-border collaboration, mutual assistance, and other cooperative agreements.**

The United States benefits from and depends upon a global network of infrastructure that enables the Nation's security and way of life. The distributed nature and interconnectedness of these assets, systems, and networks create a complex environment in which the risks the Nation faces are not distinctly contained within its borders. This is increasingly the case as services provided by critical infrastructure are often dependent on information gathered, stored, or processed in highly distributed locations. It is imperative that the government, private sector, and international partners work together. This includes collaborating to fully understand supply chain vulnerabilities and implement coordinated, and not competing, global security and resilience measures. The *National Plan* is focused on domestic efforts in critical infrastructure security and resilience, while recognizing the international aspects of the national approach.

7. **Security and resilience should be considered during the design of assets, systems, and networks.**

As critical infrastructure is built and refreshed, those involved in making design decisions, including those related to control systems, should consider the most effective and efficient ways to identify, deter, detect, disrupt, and prepare for threats and hazards; mitigate vulnerabilities; and minimize consequences. This includes considering infrastructure resilience principles.

5. Collaborating To Manage Risk

The national effort to strengthen critical infrastructure security and resilience depends on the ability of public and private sector critical infrastructure owners and operators to make risk-informed decisions on the most effective solutions available when allocating limited resources in both steady-state and crisis operations. Therefore, risk management is the cornerstone of the *National Plan* and is relevant at the national, regional, State, and local levels. National, regional, and local resilience depend upon creating and maintaining sustainable, trusted partnerships between the public and private sector. While individual entities are responsible for managing risk to their organization, partnerships improve understanding of threats, vulnerabilities, and consequences and how to manage them through the sharing of indicators and practices and the coordination of policies, response, and recovery activities.

Critical infrastructure partners manage risks based on diverse commitments to community, focus on customer welfare, and corporate governance structures. Risk tolerances will vary from organization to organization, as well as sector to sector, depending on business plans, resources, operating structure, and regulatory environments. They also differ between the private sector and the government based on underlying constraints. Different entities are likely to have different priorities with respect to security investment as well as potentially differing judgments as to what the appropriate point of risk tolerance may be. Private sector organizations generally can increase investments to meet their risk tolerances and provide for their community of stakeholders, but investments in security and resilience have legitimate limits. The government must provide for national security and public safety and operates with a different set of limits in doing so. Finding the appropriate value proposition among the partners requires understanding these differing perspectives and how they may affect efforts to set joint priorities. Within these parameters, critical infrastructure security and resilience depend on applying risk management practices of both industry and government, coupled with available resources and incentives, to guide and sustain efforts.

This section is organized based on the critical infrastructure risk management framework, introduced in the 2006 NIPP and updated in this *National Plan*. The updates help to clarify the components and streamline the steps of the framework, depicted in Figure 3 below. Specifically, the three elements of critical infrastructure (physical, cyber, and human) are explicitly identified and should be integrated throughout the steps of the framework, as appropriate. In addition, the updated framework consolidates the number of steps or "chevrons" by including prioritization with the implementation of risk management activities. Prioritization of risk mitigation options is an integral part of the decision-making process to select the risk management activities to be implemented. Finally, a reference to the feedback loop is removed and instead, the framework now depicts the importance of information sharing throughout the entire risk management process. Information is shared through each step of the framework, to include the "measure effectiveness" step, facilitating feedback and enabling continuous improvement of critical infrastructure security and resilience efforts.

Figure 3 – Critical Infrastructure Risk Management Framework

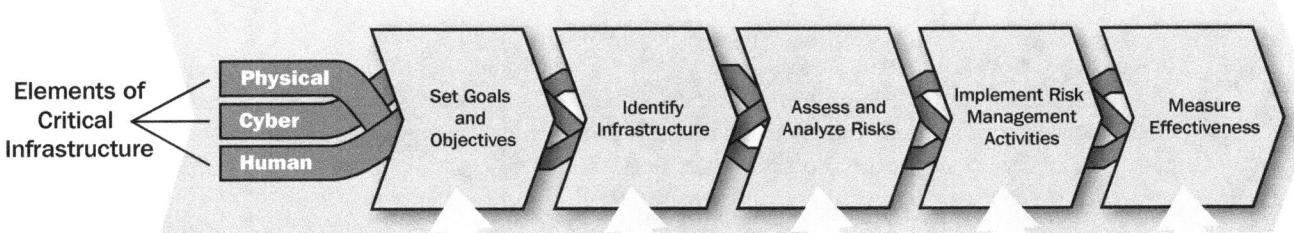

The critical infrastructure risk management framework supports a decision-making process that critical infrastructure partners collaboratively undertake to inform the selection of risk management actions. This framework is not binding and many organizations have risk management models that have proved effective and should be maintained. It does, however, provide an organizing construct for those models. This section presents a selection of risk management activities implemented across the critical infrastructure community, but the specific contributions of various partners are described where applicable. In addition, call-out boxes throughout this section identify linkages between the steps in the risk management framework and the specific actions identified in the Call to Action in section 6 of this *National Plan*.

The critical infrastructure risk management framework is designed to provide flexibility for use in all sectors, across different geographic regions, and by various partners. It can be tailored to dissimilar operating environments and applies to all threats and hazards. The risk management framework is intended to complement and support completion of the Threat and Hazard Identification and Risk Assessment (THIRA) process as conducted by regional, SLTT, and urban area jurisdictions to establish capability priorities. *Comprehensive Preparedness Guide 201: Threat and Hazard Identification and Risk Assessment, Second Edition* cites infrastructure owners and operators as sources of threat and hazard information and as valuable partners when completing the THIRA process.

The critical infrastructure community shares information throughout the steps of the risk management framework to document and build upon best practices and lessons learned and help identify and fill gaps in security and resilience efforts. It is essential for the community to share risk information, also known as risk communication, which is defined as the exchange of information with the goal of improving risk understanding, affecting risk perception, and/or equipping people or groups to act appropriately in response to an identified risk.[12]

Risk management enables the critical infrastructure community to focus on those threats and hazards that are likely to cause harm, and employ approaches that are designed to prevent or mitigate the effects of those incidents. It also increases security and strengthens resilience by identifying and prioritizing actions to ensure continuity of essential functions and services and support enhanced response and restoration.

Set Infrastructure Goals and Objectives

Set Goals and Objectives

This *National Plan* establishes a set of broad national goals for critical infrastructure security and resilience. These national goals are supported by objectives and priorities developed at the sector level, which may be articulated in Sector-Specific Plans (SSPs) and serve as targets for collaborative planning among SSAs and their sector partners in government and the private sector.

As discussed in Section 2, a set of national multi-year priorities, developed with input from all levels of the partnership, will complement these goals. These priorities might focus on particular goals or cross-sector issues where attention and resources could be applied within the critical infrastructure community with the most significant impact. Critical infrastructure owners and operators, as well as SLTT and regional entities, can identify objectives and priorities for critical infrastructure that align to these national priorities, national goals, and sector objectives, but are tailored and scaled to their operational and risk environments and available resources.

> **Related Calls to Action**
>
> • Establish National Focus through Joint Priority Setting
>
> • Determine Collective Actions through Joint Planning Efforts

Identify Infrastructure

Identify Infrastructure

To manage critical infrastructure risk effectively, partners must identify the assets, systems, and networks that are essential to their continued operation, considering associated dependencies and interdependencies. This aspect of the risk management process also should identify information and communications technologies that facilitate the provision of essential services.

Critical infrastructure partners view criticality differently, based on their unique situations, operating models, and associated risks. The Federal Government identifies and prioritizes nationally significant critical infrastructure

---

[12] U.S. Department of Homeland Security, DHS Risk Lexicon, 2010.

based upon statutory definition and national considerations.[13] SLTT governments identify and prioritize infrastructure according to their business and operating environments and associated risks. Infrastructure owners and operators identify assets, systems, and networks that are essential to their continued operations and delivery of products and services to customers. At the sector level, many SSAs collaborate with owners and operators and SLTT entities to develop lists of infrastructure that are significant at the national, regional, and local levels.

Related Call to Action

• Analyze Dependencies and Interdependencies

Effective risk management requires an understanding of criticality as well as the associated interdependencies of infrastructure. This *National Plan* identifies certain lifeline functions that are essential to the operation of most critical infrastructure sectors. These lifeline functions include communications, energy, transportation, and water. Critical infrastructure partners should identify essential functions and resources that impact their businesses and communities. The identification of these lifeline functions can support preparedness planning and capability development.

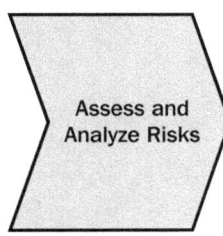

Assess and Analyze Risks

Critical infrastructure risks can be assessed in terms of the following:

• **Threat** – natural or manmade occurrence, individual, entity, or action that has or indicates the potential to harm life, information, operations, the environment, and/or property.

• **Vulnerability** – physical feature or operational attribute that renders an entity open to exploitation or susceptible to a given hazard.

• **Consequence** – effect of an event, incident, or occurrence.

Risk assessments are conducted by many critical infrastructure partners to inform their own decision making, using a broad range of methodologies. These assessments allow critical infrastructure community leaders to understand the most likely and severe incidents that could affect their operations and communities and use this information to support planning and resource allocation in a coordinated manner.

Related Call to Action

• Improve Information Sharing and Apply Knowledge to Enable Risk-informed Decision Making

To assess risk effectively, critical infrastructure partners—including owners and operators, sector councils, and government agencies—need timely, reliable, and actionable information regarding threats, vulnerabilities, and consequences. Non-governmental entities must be involved in the development and dissemination of products regarding threats, vulnerabilities, and potential consequences and provide risk information in a trusted environment. Partners should understand intelligence and information requirements and conduct joint analysis where appropriate. Critical infrastructure partnerships can bring great value in improving the understanding of risk to both cyber and physical systems and assets. Neither public nor private sector entities can fully understand risk without this integration of wide-ranging knowledge and analysis.

Supporting information-sharing initiatives exist both at the national and regional level. Information-sharing activities can protect privacy by applying the FIPPs and protect civil liberties by complying with applicable laws and policies. It is equally crucial to ensure adequate protection of sensitive business and security information that could cause serious adverse impacts to private businesses, the economy, and public or private enterprise security through unauthorized disclosure, access, or use. The Federal Government has a statutory responsibility to safeguard critical infrastructure information.[14] DHS and other agencies use the Protected Critical Infrastructure Information (PCII) program and other protocols such as Classified National Security Information, Law Enforcement Sensitive Information, and Federal Security Classification Guidelines. The PCII pro-

---

[13] The National Critical Infrastructure Prioritization Program within DHS is the primary program helping entities prioritize critical infrastructure at the national level. This program identifies nationally significant assets, systems, and networks which, if destroyed or disrupted, could cause some combination of significant casualties, major economic losses, and/or widespread and long-term impacts to national well-being and governance. Executive Order 13636 also requires DHS to use a consultative process to identify infrastructure in which a cyber incident could result in catastrophic consequences. Other Federal departments and agencies identify and prioritize their own critical infrastructure which, if destroyed or disrupted, could result in mission failure or other catastrophic consequences at the national level.
[14] Under the Homeland Security Act of 2002, §201(d)(11)(a), DHS must ensure that any material received pursuant to this Act is "protected from unauthorized disclosure and handled and used only for the performance of official duties."

---

gram, authorized by the Critical Infrastructure Information (CII) Act of 2002 and its implementing regulations (Title 6 of the Code of Federal Regulations Part 29), defines both the requirements for submitting CII and those that government agencies must follow for accessing and safeguarding CII.

Implement Risk Management Activities

Decision makers prioritize activities to manage critical infrastructure risk based on the criticality of the affected infrastructure, the costs of such activities, and the potential for risk reduction. Some risk management activities address multiple aspects of risk, while others are more targeted to address specific threats, vulnerabilities, or potential consequences. These activities can be divided into the following approaches:

Identify, Deter, Detect, Disrupt, and Prepare for Threats and Hazards

- Establish and implement joint plans and processes to evaluate needed increases in security and resilience measures, based on hazard warnings and threat reports.

- Conduct continuous monitoring of cyber systems.

- Employ security protection systems to detect or delay an attack or intrusion.

- Detect malicious activities that threaten critical infrastructure and related operational activities across the sectors.

- Implement intrusion detection or intrusion protection systems on sensitive or mission-critical networks and facilities to identify and prevent unauthorized access and exploitation.

- Monitor critical infrastructure facilities and systems potentially targeted for attack (e.g., through local law enforcement and public utilities).

Reduce Vulnerabilities

- Build security and resilience into the design and operation of assets, systems, and networks.

- Employ siting considerations when locating new infrastructure, such as avoiding floodplains, seismic zones, and other risk-prone locations.

- Develop and conduct training and exercise programs to enhance awareness and understanding of common vulnerabilities and possible mitigation strategies.

- Leverage lessons learned and apply corrective actions from incidents and exercises to enhance protective measures.

- Establish and execute business and government emergency action and continuity plans at the local and regional levels to facilitate the continued performance of critical functions during an emergency.

- Address cyber vulnerabilities through continuous diagnostics and prioritization of high-risk vulnerabilities.

- Undertake research and development efforts to reduce known cyber and physical vulnerabilities that have proved difficult or expensive to address.

Mitigate Consequences

- Share information to support situational awareness and damage assessments of cyber and physical critical infrastructure during and after an incident, including the nature and extent of the threat, cascading effects, and the status of the response.

- Work to restore critical infrastructure operations following an incident.

- Support the provision of essential services such as: emergency power to critical facilities; fuel supplies for emergency responders; and potable water, mobile communications, and food and pharmaceuticals for the affected community.

- Ensure that essential information is backed up on remote servers and that redundant processes are implemented for key functions, reducing the potential consequences of a cybersecurity incident.

- Remove key operational functions from the Internet-connected business network, reducing the likelihood that a cybersecurity incident will result in compromise of essential services.

- Ensure that incidents affecting cyber systems are fully contained; that asset, system, or network functionality is restored to pre-incident status; and that affected information is available in an uncompromised and secure state.

- Recognize and account for interdependencies in response and recovery/restoration plans.

- Repair or replace damaged infrastructure with cost-effective designs that are more secure and resilient.

- Utilize and ensure the reliability of emergency communications capabilities.

- Contribute to the development and execution of private sector, SLTT, and regional priorities for both near- and long-term recovery.

The above activities are examples of risk management activities that are being undertaken to support the overall achievement of security and resilience, whether at an organizational, community, sector, or national level. Prevention activities are most closely associated with efforts to address threats; protection efforts generally address vulnerabilities; and response and recovery efforts help minimize consequences. Mitigation efforts transcend the entire threat, vulnerability, and consequence spectrum. These five mission areas, as described in the National Preparedness Goal and System, provide a useful framework for considering risk management investments. Figure 4 illustrates the relationship of the national preparedness mission areas to the elements of risk.

The National Preparedness Goal also establishes 31 core capabilities that support the five national preparedness mission areas. The development of many of these core capabilities contributes to the achievement of critical infrastructure security and resilience and communities and owners and operators can apply these capabilities to identified activities to manage risk. Such efforts are enhanced when critical infrastructure risks are considered as part of setting capability targets.

Figure 4 – Critical Infrastructure Risk in the Context of National Preparedness

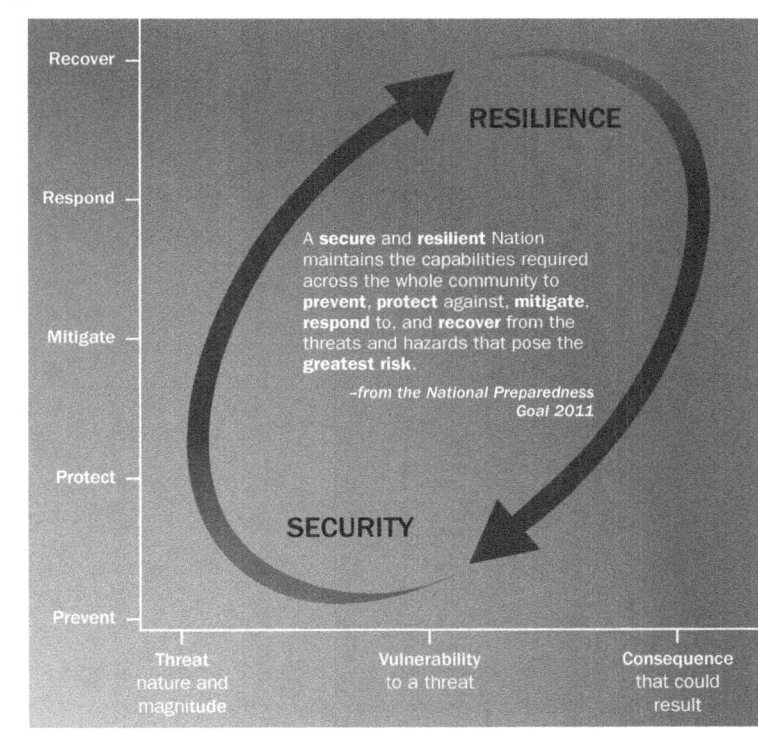

Risk Elements

To support efforts in advance of or during an incident, the critical infrastructure community collaborates based on the structures established in the National Prevention Framework, the National Protection Framework, the National Mitigation Framework, the National Response Framework (NRF), the National Disaster Recovery Framework, and the interim National Cyber Incident Response Plan or its successor.

One example of how these structures support collaborative efforts is provided through the NRF. The NRF organizational structures coordinate critical infrastructure-related activities conducted in response to a nationally declared disaster or major incident necessitating Federal assistance. Its Critical Infrastructure Support Annex[15] explains how critical infrastructure security and

---

[15] U.S. Department of Homeland Security, Critical Infrastructure Support Annex to the National Response Framework, 2013.

resilience activities are integrated into the NRF and describes policies, roles and responsibilities, incident-related actions, and coordinating structures used to assess, prioritize, secure, and restore critical infrastructure during actual or potential domestic incidents. The Annex leverages the partnership structures and information-sharing and risk management processes described in this *National Plan*. Similar linkages are in place, and will continue to be enhanced, through the other Frameworks and incident response plans.

In addition to the identified threat-, vulnerability-, and consequence-reducing activities, risk reduction can be achieved through critical infrastructure and control system design. Factoring security and resilience measures into design decisions early can facilitate integration of measures to mitigate physical and cyber vulnerabilities as well as natural and technological hazards at lower cost. Governments and businesses can better invest in measures that increase the security and resilience of both critical infrastructure and the broader society through risk analysis, evidence-based design practices, and consideration of costs and benefits. Such efforts are also helpful during infrastructure recovery efforts, in those instances when the Federal Government is working with communities and industry to rebuild infrastructure.

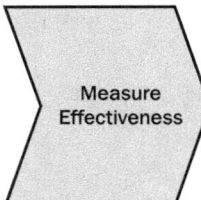

Measure Effectiveness

The critical infrastructure community evaluates the effectiveness of risk management efforts within sectors and at national, State, local, and regional levels by developing metrics for both direct and indirect indicator measurement. SSAs work with SCCs through the sector-specific planning process to develop attributes that support the national goals and national priorities as well as other sector-specific priorities. Such measures inform the risk management efforts of partners throughout the critical infrastructure community and help build a national picture of progress toward the vision of this *National Plan* as well as the National Preparedness Goal.

At a national level, the *National Plan* articulates broad area goals to achieve the *Plan's* vision that will be complemented by a set of multi-year national priorities. The critical infrastructure community will subsequently evaluate its collective progress in accomplishing the goals and priorities.

This evaluation process functions as an integrated and continuing cycle:

- Articulate the vision and national goals;

- Define national priorities;

- Identify high-level outputs or outcomes associated with the national goals and national priorities;

- Collect performance data to assess progress in achieving identified outputs and outcomes;

> **Related Calls to Action**
> - Evaluate Achievement of Goals
> - Learn and Adapt During and After Exercises and Incidents

- Evaluate progress toward achievement of the national priorities, national goals, and vision;

- Update the national priorities and adapt risk management activities accordingly; and

- Revisit the national goals and vision on a periodic basis.

Just as regular evaluation of progress toward the national goals informs the ongoing evolution of security and resilience practices, planned exercises and real-world incidents also provide opportunities for learning and adaptation. For example, fuel shortages after Hurricane Sandy illustrated the interdependencies and complexities of infrastructure systems, the challenges in achieving shared situational awareness during large events, and the need for improved information collection and sharing among government and private sector partners to support restoration activities. The critical infrastructure and national preparedness communities also conduct exercises on an ongoing basis through the National Exercise Program and other mechanisms to assess and validate the capabilities of organizations, agencies, and jurisdictions. During and after such planned and unplanned operations, partners identify individual and group weaknesses, implement and evaluate corrective actions, and share best practices with the wider critical infrastructure and emergency management communities. Such learning and adaptation inform future plans, activities, technical assistance, training, and education.

6. Call to Action: Steps to Advance The National Effort

This Call to Action guides efforts to achieve national goals aimed at enhancing national critical infrastructure security and resilience. These activities will be performed collaboratively by the critical infrastructure community.

Federal departments and agencies, engaging with SLTT, regional, and private sector partners—taking into consideration the unique risk management perspectives, priorities, and resource constraints of each sector—will work together to promote continuous improvement of security and resilience efforts to accomplish the tasks below. The actions listed in this section are not intended to be exhaustive nor is it anticipated that every sector will take every action. Instead, this section is intended as a roadmap to guide national progress while allowing for differing priorities in different sectors. As such, the actions listed below provide strategic direction for national efforts in the coming years. Call-out boxes throughout this section identify linkages between the Call to Action activities and the national goals presented in section 2.

Build upon Partnership Efforts:

1. Set National Focus through Jointly Developed Priorities

2. Determine Collective Actions through Joint Planning Efforts

3. Empower Local and Regional Partnerships to Build Capacity Nationally

4. Leverage Incentives to Advance Security and Resilience

Innovate in Managing Risk:

5. Enable Risk-Informed Decision Making through Enhanced Situational Awareness

6. Analyze Infrastructure Dependencies, Interdependencies, and Associated Cascading Effects

7. Identify, Assess, and Respond to Unanticipated Infrastructure Cascading Effects During and Following Incidents

8. Promote Infrastructure, Community, and Regional Recovery Following Incidents

9. Strengthen Coordinated Development and Delivery of Technical Assistance, Training, and Education

10. Improve Critical Infrastructure Security and Resilience by Advancing Research and Development Solutions

Focus on Outcomes:

11. Evaluate Progress toward the Achievement of Goals

12. Learn and Adapt During and After Exercises and Incidents

These actions will inform and guide efforts identified via the priority-setting and joint planning processes described below, as resources allow.

Build upon Partnership Efforts

Call to Action #1: Set National Focus through Jointly Developed Priorities

To guide national efforts and inform decisions, the national council structures will jointly set multi-year priorities and review them annually with input from all levels of the critical infrastructure community. These priorities will take into account risks facing the Nation based on the SNRA, risk assessments

Relates to All National Goals

by critical infrastructure partners, and State and regional THIRAs. Annual critical infrastructure and preparedness reporting will also inform the national priorities through assessment of capability gaps.

- Jointly establish a set of national critical infrastructure security and resilience priorities to support Federal resource allocation as well as planning and evaluation at all levels in the national partnership.

- Review and validate the national priorities on an annual basis, and update them on a regular cycle timed to inform Federal budget development and SLTT grant programs.

Call to Action #2: Determine Collective Actions through Joint Planning Efforts

Planning activities within the critical infrastructure community should reflect this *National Plan* and the joint priorities established from Call to Action #1. In particular, activities should focus on building SCC, SLTT, and regional capacity and increasing coordination with the emergency management community.

> Relates to All National Goals

- All sectors will update their Sector-Specific Plans (SSPs) to support this *National Plan*, and every four years thereafter, based on guidance developed by DHS in collaboration with the SSAs and cross-sector councils. The SSPs will:

  - Reflect joint priorities.

  - Address sector reliance on lifeline functions and include strategies to mitigate consequences from the loss of those functions, including potential cascading effects.

  - Describe approaches to integrating critical infrastructure and national preparedness efforts, in particular, transitioning from steady state to incident response and recovery via the National Response Framework's Emergency Support Functions (ESFs) and National Disaster Recovery Framework's Recovery Support Functions (RSFs).

  - Describe current and planned cybersecurity efforts, including, but not limited to, use of the Cybersecurity Framework, cybersecurity information-sharing initiatives, programmatic activities, risk assessments, exercises, incident response and recovery efforts, and any metrics.

  - Guide development of appropriate metrics and targets to measure progress toward the national goals and priorities, as well as other sector-specific priorities.

- As appropriate, SLTT and regional entities can develop supporting plans to this *National Plan* and the updated SSPs, whether cross-sector or by individual sector, that articulate shared priorities and activities at those levels. The SLTTGCC will collaborate with partners to provide guidance for such plans.

- The Federal Government will work with the critical infrastructure community to provide updated guidance on cyber incident response.

Call to Action #3: Empower Local and Regional Partnerships to Build Capacity Nationally

As most incidents are local in nature, local and regional collaboration are essential to integrating critical infrastructure security and resilience and national preparedness activities nationally. Local and regional partnerships contribute significantly to national efforts by increasing the reach of the national partnership, demonstrating its value, and advancing the national goals.

> **Related National Goal**
> - Enhance critical infrastructure resilience by minimizing adverse consequences...

- Identify existing local and regional partnerships addressing critical infrastructure security and resilience, their focus and alignment with national partnership structures, and how to engage with them. Leverage State and major urban area fusion centers to engage with local and regional partners.

- Expand a national network of critical infrastructure and SLTT partnerships and coalitions to complement and enhance the national-level focus on sectors, while remaining cognizant of varying legal structures in different jurisdictions and organizations.

- Employ the THIRA process as a method to integrate human, physical, and cyber elements of critical infrastructure risk management. Using the existing process will facilitate better coordination of planning, resource allocation, and evaluation of progress by State and local governments, as well as local infrastructure owners and operators.

- Develop and advance a joint set of regional preparedness projects demonstrating the integrated application of critical infrastructure risk management and planning. This will involve Federal agencies responsible for implementing PPD-8 and PPD-21 working collaboratively with States, metropolitan areas, rural communities, and regional coalitions.

Call to Action #4: Leverage Incentives to Advance Security and Resilience

The government and the private sector have a shared interest in ensuring the viability of critical infrastructure and the provision of essential services, under all conditions. Critical infrastructure owners and operators are often the greatest beneficiaries of investing in their own security and resilience, and are influenced by a social responsibility to adopt such practices. However, the private sector may be justifiably concerned about the return on security and resilience investments that may not yield immediately measureable benefits. Effective incentives can help justify the costs of improved security and resilience by balancing the short-term costs of additional investment with similarly near-term benefits. Market-based incentives can promote significant changes in business practices and encourage the development of markets such as insurance for cyber, chemical, biological, or radiological risks. In addition, States and localities can explore offering their own incentives to encourage investment in security and resilience measures.

> **Related National Goals**
> - Secure critical infrastructure against threats...
> - Enhance critical infrastructure resilience by minimizing adverse consequences...

- Continue to identify, analyze and, where appropriate, implement incentives.

- Support research and data gathering to quantify the potential costs imposed by a lack of critical infrastructure security and resilience, and inadequate cyber preparedness.

- Establish innovation challenge programs to incentivize new solutions to strengthen infrastructure security and resilience during infrastructure planning, design, and redesign phases, including technological, engineering, and process improvements.

Innovate in Managing Risk

Call to Action #5: Enable Risk-Informed Decision Making through Enhanced Situational Awareness

To ensure that situational awareness capabilities keep pace with a dynamic and evolving risk environment, the critical infrastructure community must continue to improve practices for sharing information and applying the knowledge gained through changes in policy, process, and culture. The community can promote a culture of "need to share" and "responsibility to provide" across all levels and sectors, recognizing that critical infrastructure owners and operators and SLTT governments are crucial consumers *and* providers of risk information. This culture is built on a shared understanding of national efforts toward greater critical infrastructure security and resilience.

> **Related National Goal**
> - Share actionable and relevant information...

Accordingly, the Federal Government will consult with SLTT governments and owners and operators to ensure that intelligence analyses meet their needs, and exercise consistent means for disseminating intelligence and information security products. It will also continue to enhance the ability of the NICC, NCCIC, and other Federal information-sharing resources to produce and share cross-sector, near real-time situational awareness while protecting sensitive information. In addition, the Federal Government will leverage "tearline" and "shareline"[16] policies and procedures to facilitate sharing of actionable portions of otherwise classified or restricted unclassified reports with private sector and SLTT partners. Likewise, State and local governments can improve information sharing between SLTT officials responsible for critical infrastructure security and resilience. State and local governments and regional partnerships can promote greater use of State and major urban area fusion centers within their respective jurisdictions and regions to inform threat identification, risk assessment, and priority development. Owners and operators can support improvements by giving government intelligence analysts ongoing feedback on information needs and the dissemination and application of their information products and by sharing information with Federal and SLTT governments.

---

[16] "Tearlines" are portions of an intelligence report or product that provide the substance of a more classified or controlled report without identifying sources, methods, or other operational information. Tearlines release classified intelligence information with less restrictive dissemination controls, and, when possible, at a lower classification; "shareline" refers to an unclassified and less restrictive portion or excerpt of a report or other information source that provides the substance of a dissemination-controlled report.

- Undertake a partnership-wide review of impediments to information sharing to support efforts to address those challenges and develop best practices. Analyze legal considerations, the classification or sensitive nature of certain information, laws and policies that govern information dissemination, and the need to build trust among partners.

- Build upon the functional relationship descriptions developed as part of PPD-21 by further analyzing functional relationships within and across the Federal Government (focused on critical infrastructure security and resilience) to identify overlaps, inefficiencies, and gaps and recommend changes to enhance situational awareness and risk-informed decision making.

- Develop streamlined, standardized processes to promote integration and coordination of information sharing via jointly developed doctrine and supporting standard operating procedures.

- Develop interoperability standards to enable more efficient information exchange through defined data standards and requirements, to include (1) a foundation for an information-sharing environment that has common data requirements and information flow and exchange across entities; and (2) sector-specific critical information requirements (i.e., critical reporting criteria), to allow for improved information flow and reporting to produce more complete and timely situational awareness for security and resilience.

Call to Action #6: Analyze Infrastructure Dependencies, Interdependencies, and Associated Cascading Effects

Greater analysis of dependencies and interdependencies at international, national, regional, and local levels can inform planning and facilitate prioritization of resources to ensure the continuity of critical services and mitigate the cascading impacts of incidents that do occur.

> **Related National Goal**
> - Assess and analyze threats, vulnerabilities, and consequences...

- Mature the capability to identify and understand cross-sector physical and cyber dependencies and interdependencies over different time frames at international, national, regional, and local levels. Focus on the lifeline functions and the resilience of global supply chains during potentially high-consequence incidents, given their importance to public health, welfare, and economic activity.

- Continue to evolve the Cyber-Dependent Infrastructure Identification approach under Executive Order 13636 to consider the potential risks resulting from dependency on information and communications technology and inform preparedness planning and capability development.

Call to Action #7: Identify, Assess, and Respond to Unanticipated Infrastructure Cascading Effects During and Following Incidents

Critical infrastructure and emergency response planning and exercises, as well as real-world events, underscore the need to prepare for cascading effects during incidents that could potentially magnify consequences. The critical infrastructure community can significantly help the Nation prepare for all-hazard incidents by developing the capability to rapidly identify, assess, and respond to cascading effects, beginning with the lifeline functions, during and following incidents.

> **Related National Goal**
> - Enhance critical infrastructure resilience by minimizing adverse consequences...

- Enhance the capability to rapidly identify and assess cascading effects involving the lifeline functions and contribute to identifying infrastructure priorities—both known and emerging—during response and recovery efforts.

- Enhance the capacity of critical infrastructure partners to work through incident management structures such as the ESFs to mitigate the consequences of disruptions to the lifeline functions.

Call to Action #8: Promote Infrastructure, Community, and Regional Recovery Following Incidents

Recent incidents highlight the need for long-term recovery capabilities to enhance the security and resilience of infrastructure, communities, and regions during rebuilding. To develop such capabilities, critical infrastructure partners can leverage existing trust relationships and engage a spectrum of whole community partners active in recovery, including citizens, non-profits, business leaders, and government representatives not usually involved in infrastructure or security discussions.

> **Related National Goal**
> - Enhance critical infrastructure resilience by minimizing adverse consequences...

- Leverage Federal field staff (including Protective Security Advisors) and encourage States and localities to promote consideration of critical infrastructure challenges in pre-incident recovery planning, post-incident damage assessments, and development of recovery strategies.

- Support examination of initiatives to enhance, repair, or replace infrastructure providing lifeline functions during recovery.

Call to Action #9: Strengthen Coordinated Development and Delivery of Technical Assistance, Training, and Education

To continue to execute and sustain risk management activities and prepare organizations and professionals to meet future challenges, the critical infrastructure community must continue to develop and deliver innovative technical assistance, training, and education programs and assess their effectiveness.

> **Related National Goal**
>
> - Promote learning and adaptation during and after exercises and incidents...

- Capture, report, and prioritize the technical assistance, training, and education needs of the various partners within the critical infrastructure community.

- Examine current Federal technical assistance, training, and education programs to ensure that they support the national priorities and the risk management activities described in this *National Plan* in order to advance progress toward the national goals.

- Increase coordination of technical assistance efforts—particularly within DHS and among the SSAs—and leverage a wider network of partners to deliver training and education programs to better serve recipients and reach a wider audience while conserving resources.

- Partner with academia to establish and update critical infrastructure curricula that help to train critical infrastructure professionals, including executives and managers, to manage the benefits and inherent vulnerabilities introduced by information and communications technologies in critical infrastructure assets, systems, and networks.

Call to Action #10: Improve Critical Infrastructure Security and Resilience by Advancing Research and Development Solutions

PPD-21 directs the Federal Government to provide a research and development (R&D) plan that takes into account the evolving threat landscape, annual metrics, and other relevant information to identify priorities and guide research and development requirements and investments. The *National Critical Infrastructure Security and Resilience R&D Plan* will be reissued every four years, with interim updates as needed. It will focus on the following:

> **Related National Goals**
>
> - Secure critical infrastructure against threats...
>
> - Enhance critical infrastructure resilience by minimizing adverse consequences...

- Promoting R&D to enable the secure and resilient design and construction of critical infrastructure and more secure accompanying cyber technology;

- Enhancing modeling capabilities to determine potential impacts on critical infrastructure of an incident or threat scenario, as well as cascading effects on other sectors;

- Facilitating initiatives to incentivize cybersecurity investments and the adoption of critical infrastructure design features that strengthen all-hazards security and resilience; and

- Prioritizing efforts to support the strategic guidance issued by DHS.

To increase infrastructure security and resilience, R&D requires coordination to address analytic and policy capability gaps, improve risk management capabilities for owners and operators, and execute and transition R&D into operational use. R&D must address protection of existing critical infrastructure as well as the design and construction of new infrastructure to include interdependencies. Priorities may emerge from the R&D requirements of the 16 sectors, both from commonly embraced requirements, and from discrete requirements that provide the greatest potential return. The *National Critical Infrastructure Security and Resilience R&D Plan* will incorporate sector-specific R&D planning documents that address needs and priorities from the perspective of the sectors.

Call to Action #11: Evaluate Progress Toward the Achievement of Goals

While much of the groundwork for the integrated evaluation cycle described in section 5 already exists, critical infrastructure partners should participate on a wider and more consistent scale to facilitate understanding of progress and adaptive decision making.

> **Related National Goal**
> • Promote learning and adaptation during and after exercises and incidents...

- Jointly identify high-level outputs or outcomes associated with the national goals and priorities to facilitate evaluation of progress toward the goals and priorities.

- Develop the Critical Infrastructure National Annual Report and National Preparedness Report annually through standardized data calls to SSAs and sector partners to build a national picture of progress toward the *National Plan's* vision and goals and the National Preparedness Goal. Incorporate performance data from industry, SLTT, and regional entities to reflect progress throughout the critical infrastructure community at all levels.

Call to Action #12: Learn and Adapt During and After Exercises and Incidents

Given the evolving nature of threats and hazards, the national aspiration of secure and resilient critical infrastructure is achievable only through the collective efforts of numerous partners grounded in continuous learning and adaptation to changing environments. The critical infrastructure community can better realize the opportunities for learning and adaptation during and after exercises and incidents through more collaborative exercise design, coordinated lessons learned and corrective action processes, and streamlined sharing of best practices.

- Develop and conduct exercises through participatory processes to suit diverse needs and purposes.

> **Related National Goal**
> • Promote learning and adaptation during and after exercises and incidents...

  - Promote broad participation and coordination among government and interested private sector partners—including the R&D community—in exercise design, conduct, and evaluation to reflect the perspectives of all partners and maximize the value for future planning and operations.

  - Develop exercises at multiple levels and in various formats to suit national, regional, and SLTT needs.

- Design exercises to reflect lessons learned and test corrective actions from previous exercises and incidents, address both physical and cyber threats and vulnerabilities, and evaluate the transition from steady state to incident response and recovery efforts.

- Share lessons learned and corrective actions from exercises and incidents and rapidly incorporate them into technical assistance, training, and education programs to improve future security and resilience efforts.

The actions listed in this section are not intended to be exhaustive, but rather to help focus the critical infrastructure community to advance the national effort toward security and resilience. Through coordinated and flexible implementation by Federal departments and agencies—as well as SLTT, regional, and private sector partners as appropriate, given their unique risk management perspectives—these actions will enable continuous improvement of security and resilience efforts to address both familiar and novel challenges.

> More information about the NIPP is available on the Internet at: **www.dhs.gov/nipp**

Acronyms

CDII	Cyber Dependent Infrastructure Identification
CII	Critical Infrastructure Information
CIPAC	Critical Infrastructure Partnership Advisory Council
DHS	Department of Homeland Security
EO	Executive Order
ESF	Emergency Support Function
FACA	Federal Advisory Committee Act
FBI	Federal Bureau of Investigation
FEMA	Department of Homeland Security/Federal Emergency Management Agency
FSLC	Federal Senior Leadership Council
GCC	Government Coordinating Council
ISAC	Information Sharing and Analysis Center
JTTF	Joint Terrorism Task Force
NCCIC	National Cybersecurity and Communications Integration Center
NCIJTF	National Cyber Investigative Joint Task Force
NCIPP	National Critical Infrastructure Prioritization Program
NICC	National Infrastructure Coordinating Center
NIPP	National Infrastructure Protection Plan
NOC	National Operations Center
NRF	National Response Framework
PCII	Protected Critical Infrastructure Information
PNT	Positioning, Navigation, and Timing
PPD	Presidential Policy Directive
R&D	Research and Development
RC3	Regional Consortium Coordinating Council

RSF	Recovery Support Function
SCADA	Supervisory Control and Data Acquisition
SCC	Sector Coordinating Council
SLTT	State, Local, Tribal, and Territorial
SLTTGCC	State, Local, Tribal, and Territorial Government Coordinating Council
SNRA	Strategic National Risk Assessment
SOP	Standard Operating Procedure
SSA	Sector-Specific Agency
SSP	Sector-Specific Plan
THIRA	Threat and Hazard Identification and Risk Assessment
U.S.	United States
U.S.C.	United States Code

Glossary of Terms

Many of the definitions in this Glossary are derived from language enacted in Federal laws and/or included in national plans, including the Homeland Security Act of 2002; the USA PATRIOT Act of 2001; the 2009 NIPP; Presidential Policy Directive (PPD) 8, National Preparedness; and PPD-21, Critical Infrastructure Security and Resilience. Additional definitions come from the DHS Lexicon. The source for each entry below follows each definition. For purposes of this National Plan, these definitions apply.

All Hazards. The term "all hazards" means a threat or an incident, natural or manmade, that warrants action to protect life, property, the environment, and public health or safety, and to minimize disruptions of government, social, or economic activities. It includes natural disasters, cyber incidents, industrial accidents, pandemics, acts of terrorism, sabotage, and destructive criminal activity targeting critical infrastructure. (Source: PPD-21, 2013)

Asset. Person, structure, facility, information, material, or process that has value. (Source: DHS Lexicon, 2010)

Business Continuity. Activities performed by an organization to ensure that during and after a disaster the organization's essential functions are maintained uninterrupted, or are resumed with minimal disruption. (Source: Adapted from the 2009 NIPP)

Consequence. The effect of an event, incident, or occurrence, including the number of deaths, injuries, and other human health impacts along with economic impacts both direct and indirect and other negative outcomes to society. (Source: Adapted from DHS Lexicon, 2010)

Control Systems. Computer-based systems used within many infrastructure and industries to monitor and control sensitive processes and physical functions. These systems typically collect measurement and operational data from the field, process and display the information, and relay control commands to local or remote equipment or human-machine interfaces (operators). Examples of types of control systems include SCADA systems, Process Control Systems, and Distributed Control Systems. (Source: 2009 NIPP)

Critical Infrastructure. Systems and assets, whether physical or virtual, so vital to the United States that the incapacity or destruction of such systems and assets would have a debilitating impact on security, national economic security, national public health or safety, or any combination of those matters. (Source: §1016(e) of the USA Patriot Act of 2001 (42 U.S.C. §5195c(e))

Critical Infrastructure Community. Critical infrastructure owners and operators, both public and private; Federal departments and agencies; regional entities; SLTT governments; and other organizations from the private and nonprofit sectors with a role in securing and strengthening the resilience of the Nation's critical infrastructure and/or promoting practices and ideas for doing so. (Source: NIPP 2013: *Partnering for Critical Infrastructure Security and Resilience*)

Critical Infrastructure Cross-Sector Council. Private sector council that comprises the chairs and vice chairs of the SCCs. This council coordinates cross-sector issues, initiatives, and interdependencies to support critical infrastructure security and resilience. (Source: Adapted from the 2009 NIPP)

Critical Infrastructure Information (CII). Information that is not customarily in the public domain and is related to the security of critical infrastructure or protected systems. CII consists of records and information concerning any of the following:

- Actual, potential, or threatened interference with, attack on, compromise of, or incapacitation of critical infrastructure or protected systems by either physical or computer-based attack or other similar conduct (including the misuse of or unauthorized access to all types of communications and data transmission systems) that violates Federal, State, or local law; harms the interstate commerce of the United States; or threatens public health or safety.

- The ability of any critical infrastructure or protected system to resist such interference, compromise, or incapacitation, including any planned or past assessment, projection, or estimate of the vulnerability of critical infrastructure or a protected system, including security testing, risk evaluation, risk management planning, or risk audit.

- Any planned or past operational problem or solution regarding critical infrastructure or protected systems, including repair, recovery, insurance, or continuity, to the extent that it is related to such interference, compromise, or incapacitation. (Source: CII Act of 2002, 6 U.S.C. § 131)

Critical Infrastructure Owners and Operators. Those entities responsible for day-to-day operation and investment of a particular critical infrastructure entity. (Source: Adapted from the 2009 NIPP)

Critical Infrastructure Partner. Those Federal and SLTT governmental entities, public and private sector owners and operators and representative organizations, regional organizations and coalitions, academic and professional entities, and certain not-for-profit and private volunteer organizations that share responsibility for securing and strengthening the resilience of the Nation's critical infrastructure. (Source: Adapted from the 2009 NIPP)

Critical Infrastructure Partnership Advisory Council (CIPAC). Council established by DHS under 6 U.S.C. §451 to facilitate effective interaction and coordination of critical infrastructure activities among the Federal Government; the private sector; and SLTT governments. (Source: CIPAC Charter)

Critical Infrastructure Risk Management Framework. A planning and decision-making framework that outlines the process for setting goals and objectives, identifying infrastructure, assessing risks, implementing risk management activities, and measuring effectiveness to inform continuous improvement in critical infrastructure security and resilience. (Source: Adapted from the 2009 NIPP)

Cybersecurity. The prevention of damage to, unauthorized use of, or exploitation of, and, if needed, the restoration of electronic information and communications systems and the information contained therein to ensure confidentiality, integrity, and availability; includes protection and restoration, when needed, of information networks and wireline, wireless, satellite, public safety answering points, and 911 communications systems and control systems. (Source: 2009 NIPP)

Cyber System. Any combination of facilities, equipment, personnel, procedures, and communications integrated to provide cyber services; examples include business systems, control systems, and access control systems. (Source: 2009 NIPP)

Dependency. The one-directional reliance of an asset, system, network, or collection thereof—within or across sectors—on an input, interaction, or other requirement from other sources in order to function properly. (Source: 2009 NIPP)

Executive Order 13636. Executive Order that calls for the Federal Government to closely coordinate with critical infrastructure owners and operators to improve cybersecurity information sharing; develop a technology-neutral cybersecurity framework; and promote and incentivize the adoption of strong cybersecurity practices. (Executive Order 13636,[17] *Improving Critical Infrastructure Cybersecurity,* February 2013)

Emergency Support Functions (ESF). The primary, but not exclusive, Federal coordinating structures for building, sustaining, and delivering the response core capabilities. ESFs are vital for responding to Stafford Act incidents but also may be used for other incidents. (Source: National Response Framework, 2013)

Federal Departments and Agencies. Any authority of the United States that is an "agency" under 44 U.S.C. §3502(1), other than those considered to be independent regulatory agencies, as defined in 44 U.S.C. §3502(5). (Source: PPD-21, 2013)

Function. Service, process, capability, or operation performed by an asset, system, network, or organization. (Source: DHS Lexicon, 2010)

Fusion Center. A State and major urban area focal point for the receipt, analysis, gathering, and sharing of threat-related information between the Federal Government, SLTT, and private sector partners. (Source: Adapted from the DHS Lexicon, 2010)

Government Coordinating Council (GCC). The government counterpart to the Sector Coordinating Council for each sector, established to enable interagency and intergovernmental coordination; comprises representatives across various levels of government (Federal and SLTT) as appropriate to the risk and operational landscape of each sector. (Source: 2009 NIPP)

---

[17] Executive Order 13636, http://www.gpo.gov/fdsys/pkg/FR-2013-02-19/pdf/2013-03915.pdf

Hazard. Natural or manmade source or cause of harm or difficulty. (Source: DHS Lexicon, 2010)

Incident. An occurrence, caused by either human action or natural phenomenon, that may cause harm and require action, which can include major disasters, emergencies, terrorist attacks, terrorist threats, wild and urban fires, floods, hazardous materials spills, nuclear accidents, aircraft accidents, earthquakes, hurricanes, tornadoes, tropical storms, war-related disasters, public health and medical emergencies, cyber attacks, cyber failure/accident, and other occurrences requiring an emergency response. (Source: DHS Lexicon, 2010)

Information Sharing and Analysis Centers (ISACs). Operational entities formed by critical infrastructure owners and operators to gather, analyze, appropriately sanitize, and disseminate intelligence and information related to critical infrastructure. ISACs provide 24/7 threat warning and incident reporting capabilities and have the ability to reach and share information within their sectors, between sectors, and among government and private sector stakeholders. (Source: Presidential Decision Directive 63, 1998)

Information Sharing and Analysis Organization. Any formal or informal entity or collaboration created or employed by public or private sector organizations, for purposes of:

(a) Gathering and analyzing critical infrastructure information in order to better understand security problems and interdependencies related to critical infrastructure and protected systems, so as to ensure the availability, integrity, and reliability thereof;

(b) Communicating or disclosing critical infrastructure information to help prevent, detect, mitigate, or recover from the effects of an interference, compromise, or an incapacitation problem related to critical infrastructure or protected systems; and

(c) Voluntarily disseminating critical infrastructure information to its members, State, local, and Federal Governments, or any other entities that may be of assistance in carrying out the purposes specified in subparagraphs (a) and (b). (Source: Homeland Security Act of 2002, 6 U.S.C. § 131)

Infrastructure. The framework of interdependent networks and systems comprising identifiable industries, institutions (including people and procedures), and distribution capabilities that provide a reliable flow of products and services essential to the defense and economic security of the United States, the smooth functioning of government at all levels, and society as a whole; consistent with the definition in the Homeland Security Act, infrastructure includes physical, cyber, and/or human elements. (Source: DHS Lexicon, 2010)

Interdependency. Mutually reliant relationship between entities (objects, individuals, or groups); the degree of interdependency does not need to be equal in both directions. (Source: DHS Lexicon, 2010)

Joint Terrorism Task Forces (JTTFs). FBI-led local task forces of highly trained Federal, State, and local law enforcement and intelligence agencies established to collect terrorism-related intelligence and conduct investigations. The local FBI JTTFs receive and resolve reports of possible terrorism activity submitted by private industry partners and the public. (Source: Federal Bureau of Investigation, 2013)

Mitigation. Capabilities necessary to reduce loss of life and property by lessening the impact of disasters. (Source: PPD-8, 2011)

National Cyber Investigative Joint Task Force. The multi-agency national focal point for coordinating, integrating, and sharing pertinent information related to cyber threat investigations, with representation from Federal agencies, including DHS, and from State, local, and international law enforcement partners. (Source: FBI Web site, www.fbi.gov)

National Cybersecurity and Communications Integration Center. The national cyber critical infrastructure center, as designated by the Secretary of Homeland Security, which secures Federal civilian agencies in cyberspace; provides support and expertise to private sector partners and SLTT entities; coordinates with international partners; and coordinates the Federal Government mitigation and recovery efforts for significant cyber and communications incidents. (Source: DHS Web site, www.dhs.gov)

National Infrastructure Coordinating Center. The national physical critical infrastructure center, as designated by the Secretary of Homeland Security, which coordinates a national network dedicated to the security and resilience of critical infrastructure of the United States by providing 24/7 situational awareness through information sharing, and fostering a unity of effort. (Source: DHS Web site, www.dhs.gov)

National Operations Center. A DHS 24/7 operations center responsible for providing real-time situational awareness and monitoring of the homeland, coordinating incident response activities, and, in conjunction with the Office of Intelligence and Analysis, issuing advisories and bulletins concerning threats to homeland security, as well as specific protective measures. (Source: DHS Web site, www.dhs.gov)

National Preparedness. The actions taken to plan, organize, equip, train, and exercise to build and sustain the capabilities necessary to prevent, protect against, mitigate the effects of, respond to, and recover from those threats that pose the greatest risk to the security of the Nation. (Source: PPD-8, 2011)

Network. A group of components that share information or interact with each other to perform a function. (Source: 2009 NIPP)

Partnership. Close cooperation between parties having common interests in achieving a shared vision. (Source: NIPP 2013: *Partnering for Critical Infrastructure Security and Resilience*)

Presidential Policy Directive 8 (PPD-8). Facilitates an integrated, all-of-Nation approach to national preparedness for the threats that pose the greatest risk to the security of the Nation, including acts of terrorism, cyber attacks, pandemics, and catastrophic natural disasters; directs the Federal Government to develop a national preparedness system to build and improve the capabilities necessary to maintain national preparedness across the five mission areas covered in the PPD: prevention, protection, mitigation, response, and recovery. (Source: PPD-8, 2011)

Presidential Policy Directive 21 (PPD-21). Aims to clarify roles and responsibilities across the Federal Government and establish a more effective partnership with owners and operators and SLTT entities to enhance the security and resilience of critical infrastructure. (Source: PPD-21,[18] 2013)

Prevention. Those capabilities necessary to avoid, prevent, or stop a threatened or actual act of terrorism. (Source: PPD-8, 2011)

Protected Critical Infrastructure Information (PCII). All critical infrastructure information that has been properly submitted and validated pursuant to the Critical Infrastructure Information Act and implementing directive; all information submitted to the PCII Program Office or designee with an express statement is presumed to be PCII until the PCII Program Office determines otherwise. (Source: CII Act of 2002, 6 U.S.C. § 131)

Protection. Those capabilities necessary to secure the homeland against acts of terrorism and manmade or natural disasters. (Source: PPD-8, 2011)

Recovery. Those capabilities necessary to assist communities affected by an incident to recover effectively, including, but not limited to, rebuilding infrastructure systems; providing adequate interim and long-term housing for survivors; restoring health, social, and community services; promoting economic development; and restoring natural and cultural resources. (Source: PPD-8, 2011)

Recovery Support Functions (RSF). Coordinating structures for key functional areas of assistance during recovery operations; RSFs support local governments by facilitating problem solving, improving access to resources, and fostering coordination among State and Federal agencies, nongovernmental partners, and stakeholders. (Source: National Disaster Recovery Framework, 2011)

Regional. Entities and interests spanning geographic areas ranging from large multi-State areas to metropolitan areas and varying by organizational structure and key initiatives, yet fostering engagement and collaboration between critical infrastructure owners and operators, government, and other key stakeholders within the given location. (Source: *Regional Partnerships: Enabling Regional Critical Infrastructure Resilience*, RC3, March 2011)

Regional Consortium Coordinating Council. Comprises regional groups and coalitions around the country engaged in various initiatives to advance critical infrastructure security and resilience in the public and private sectors. (Source: Adapted from the 2009 NIPP)

Resilience. The ability to prepare for and adapt to changing conditions and withstand and recover rapidly from disruptions; includes the ability to withstand and recover from deliberate attacks, accidents, or naturally occurring threats or incidents. (Source: PPD-21, 2013)

---

[18] The White House, Presidential Policy Directive 21 – Critical Infrastructure Security and Resilience, http://www.whitehouse.gov/the-press-office/2013/02/12/presidential-policy-directive-critical-infrastructure-security-and-resil

Response. Capabilities necessary to save lives, protect property and the environment, and meet basic human needs after an incident has occurred. (Source: PPD-8, 2011)

Risk. The potential for an unwanted outcome resulting from an incident, event, or occurrence, as determined by its likelihood and the associated consequences. (Source: DHS Lexicon, 2010)

Risk-Informed Decision Making. The determination of a course of action predicated on the assessment of risk, the expected impact of that course of action on that risk, and other relevant factors. (Source: 2009 NIPP)

Sector. A logical collection of assets, systems, or networks that provide a common function to the economy, government, or society; the *National Plan* addresses 16 critical infrastructure sectors, as identified in PPD-21. (Source: Adapted from the 2009 NIPP)

Sector Coordinating Council (SCC). The private sector counterpart to the GCC, these councils are self-organized, self-run, and self-governed organizations that are representative of a spectrum of key stakeholders within a sector; serve as principal entry points for the government to collaborate with each sector for developing and coordinating a wide range of critical infrastructure security and resilience activities and issues. (Source: Adapted from the 2009 NIPP)

Sector-Specific Agency (SSA). A Federal department or agency designated by PPD-21 with responsibility for providing institutional knowledge and specialized expertise as well as leading, facilitating, or supporting the security and resilience programs and associated activities of its designated critical infrastructure sector in the all-hazards environment. (Source: PPD-21, 2013)

Sector-Specific Plans (SSP). Planning documents that complement and tailor application of the *National Plan* to the specific characteristics and risk landscape of each critical infrastructure sector; developed by the SSAs in close collaboration with the SCCs and other sector partners. (Source: Adapted from the 2009 NIPP)

Secure/Security. Reducing the risk to critical infrastructure by physical means or defens[ive] cyber measures to intrusions, attacks, or the effects of natural or manmade disasters. (Source: PPD-21, 2013)

Steady State. The posture for routine, normal, day-to-day operations as contrasted with temporary periods of heightened alert or real-time response to threats or incidents. (Source: DHS Lexicon, 2010)

System. Any combination of facilities, equipment, personnel, procedures, and communications integrated for a specific purpose. (Source: DHS Lexicon, 2010)

Terrorism. Premeditated threat or act of violence against noncombatant persons, property, and environmental or economic targets to induce fear, intimidate, coerce, or affect a government, the civilian population, or any segment thereof, in furtherance of political, social, ideological, or religious objectives. (Source: DHS Lexicon, 2010)

Threat. A natural or manmade occurrence, individual, entity, or action that has or indicates the potential to harm life, information, operations, the environment, and/or property. (Source: DHS Lexicon, 2010)

Threat and Hazard Identification and Risk Assessment (THIRA). A tool that allows a regional, State, or urban area jurisdiction to understand its threats and hazards and how the impacts may vary according to time of occurrence, season, location, and other community factors. This knowledge helps a jurisdiction establish informed and defensible capability targets for preparedness. (Source: FEMA Web site, www.fema.gov)

Value Proposition. A statement that outlines the business and national interest in critical infrastructure security and resilience actions and articulates the benefits gained by partners through collaborating in the mechanisms described in the *National Plan*. (Source: Adapted from the 2009 NIPP)

Vulnerability. A physical feature or operational attribute that renders an entity open to exploitation or susceptible to a given hazard. (Source: DHS Lexicon, 2010)

Appendix A. The National Partnership Structure

The mechanisms for collaboration between private sector owners and operators and government agencies were first established through the NIPP and further refined by PPD-21, which organized the Nation's critical infrastructure into 16 sectors, identified Sector-Specific Agencies (SSAs) for each of the sectors, and established the requirement for partnerships of the Federal Government, critical infrastructure owners and operators, and State, local, tribal, and territorial (SLTT) government entities. This sector and cross-sector partnership council structure—consisting of Sector Coordinating Councils (SCCs), Government Coordinating Councils (GCCs), SSAs, and cross-sector councils—brings together partners from Federal and SLTT governments, regional entities, the private sector, and non-governmental organizations to collaborate on critical infrastructure security and resilience programs and approaches, and to achieve national goals and objectives. These councils provide primary organizational structures for coordinating critical infrastructure security and resilience efforts and activities within and across the 16 sectors.

Sector Coordinating Structures

The public-private coordination for critical infrastructure security and resilience is built through the joint efforts of multiple components of the critical infrastructure sector partnership, including SCCs, GCCs, cross-sector councils, and SSAs. Each of these components serves interests within its own constituency in addition to providing an interface with its partners. The unique features of these elements of the partnership are presented below.

Sector Coordinating Councils – The SCCs are self-organized, self-run, and self-governed councils that enable owners and operators, their trade associations, vendors, and others to interact on a wide range of sector-specific strategies, policies, activities, and issues. The SCCs serve as sector policy coordination and planning entities to collaborate with SSAs and related GCCs to address the entire range of critical infrastructure security and resilience activities and issues for that sector. As such, they serve as a voice for the sector and represent principal entry points for the government to collaborate with the sector for critical infrastructure security and resilience activities. In addition, the SCCs are encouraged to participate in efforts to establish voluntary practices to ensure that sector perspectives are included.

Other primary functions of an SCC may include the following:

- Serve as a strategic communication and coordination mechanism between owners, operators, and suppliers, and, as appropriate, with the government during emerging threats or response and recovery operations, as determined by the sector;

- Identify, implement, and support appropriate information-sharing capabilities and mechanisms in sectors where no information-sharing structure exists;

- Encourage representative membership of the sector;

- Participate in planning efforts related to the revision of the *National Plan* and development and revision of Sector-Specific Plans (SSPs), and review the annual submission to DHS on sector activities;

- Facilitate inclusive organization and coordination of the sector's policy development regarding critical infrastructure security and resilience planning and preparedness, exercises and training, public awareness, and associated implementation activities and requirements;

- Identify, develop, and share information with the sector, both public and private sector members, concerning effective cyber-security practices, such as cybersecurity working groups, risk assessments, strategies, and plans;

- Understand and communicate requirements of the sector for government support; and

- Provide input to the government on sector R&D efforts and requirements.

Government Coordinating Councils – The GCCs enable interagency, intergovernmental, and cross-jurisdictional coordination within and across sectors. They comprise representatives from across various levels of government (Federal and SLTT), as appropriate to the operating landscape of each individual sector. Each GCC is chaired by a representative from the designated SSA with responsibility for ensuring appropriate representation on the council and providing cross-sector coordination with SLTT governments. The Assistant Secretary for Infrastructure Protection or his/her designee co-chairs all GCCs. The GCC coordinates strategies, activities, policies, and communications across governmental entities within each sector. Reaching across the partnership, the GCC works to coordinate with and support the efforts of the SCC.

Other primary functions of a GCC may include the following:

- Provide interagency strategic communications and coordination at the sector level through partnership with DHS, the SSA, and other supporting agencies across various levels of government;

- Participate in planning efforts related to the revision of the *National Plan* and the development and revision of SSPs;

- Coordinate strategic communications and discussion and resolution of issues among government entities within the sector;

- Promote adoption of physical and cyber risk management processes across the sector;

- Enhance government information sharing across the sector and promote multichannel public-private information sharing;

- Identify and support the information-sharing capabilities and mechanisms that are most appropriate for SLTT entities; and

- Coordinate with and support the efforts of the SCC to plan, implement, and execute the Nation's critical infrastructure security and resilience mission.

Sector-Specific Agencies – Recognizing existing statutory or regulatory authorities of specific Federal departments and agencies, and leveraging existing sector familiarity and relationships, SSAs serve as a Federal interface for the prioritization and coordination of sector-specific security and resilience efforts and carry out incident management responsibilities for their sectors. For sectors subject to Federal or State regulation, the SSA collaborates with the regulator, as appropriate. SSAs promote sector-wide information sharing and support the national program by addressing joint national priorities and reporting on progress toward achieving security and resilience outcomes. Appendix B provides more detail on the specific roles and responsibilities of SSAs.

Cross-Sector Coordinating Structures

The NIPP establishes four principal cross-sector councils to participate in planning efforts related to the development of national priorities and related policy and planning documents that guide critical infrastructure security and resilience efforts at the national level, including this *National Plan*. All the cross-sector councils will have charters that include bylaws; these documents will be publicly available to ensure transparent governance. Each of these councils is described below.

Critical Infrastructure Cross-Sector Council – The Critical Infrastructure Cross-Sector Council provides a forum for SCCs to address cross-sector issues and interdependencies. The Council is composed of the chairs and vice chairs of the SCCs or their official designees. The members of the Council may choose to designate or appoint a Council Chair and Vice Chair.[19] The primary activities of the Council include:

- Providing senior-level, cross-sector strategic and policy coordination through partnership with DHS, the FSLC, SLTTGCC, and RC3;

- Identifying and disseminating critical infrastructure security and resilience best practices across the sectors;

[19] At the request of the Critical Infrastructure Cross-Sector Council, DHS may work with the Council to provide coordination or Secretariat support as needed.

- Identifying areas where cross-sector collaboration could advance national priorities; and

- Participating in the development and implementation of the *National Plan*.

Federal Senior Leadership Council (FSLC) – The FSLC is composed of senior officials from the designated SSAs and other Federal departments and agencies identified in PPD-21. The FSLC facilitates enhanced Federal communication and coordination across the sectors focused on critical infrastructure security and resilience. The Council's primary activities include:

- Forging consensus on risk management strategies;

- Evaluating and promoting implementation of risk-informed critical infrastructure security and resilience programs;

- Coordinating strategic issues and issue management resolution among the SLTTGCC, Critical Infrastructure Cross-Sector Council, and RC3;

- Advancing collaboration within and across sectors and with the international community;

- Advocating for and tracking execution of the *National Plan* across the Executive Branch;

- Supporting development of resource requests to fulfill the Federal mission; and

- Evaluating and reporting on the progress of Federal critical infrastructure security and resilience activities.

State, Local, Tribal, and Territorial Government Coordinating Council (SLTTGCC) – The SLTTGCC serves as a forum to promote the engagement of SLTT partners as active participants in national critical infrastructure security and resilience efforts and to provide an organizational structure to coordinate across jurisdictions on SLTT government-level guidance, strategies, and programs. The SLTTGCC:

- Provides senior-level, cross-jurisdictional strategic communications and coordination through partnership with the Federal Government and critical infrastructure owners and operators;

- Coordinates strategic issues and issue management resolution among Federal departments and agencies and SLTT partners;

- Coordinates with the FSLC, Critical Infrastructure Cross-Sector Council, and RC3 to support efforts to plan, implement, and execute the Nation's critical infrastructure security and resilience mission;

- Provides DHS with information on SLTT-level security and resilience initiatives, activities, and best practices; and

- Cooperates with DHS in establishing test sites for demonstration projects to support innovation.

Regional Consortium Coordinating Council (RC3) – The RC3 provides a framework that supports existing regional groups in their efforts to promote resilience activities in the public and private sectors. Composed of a variety of regional groups from around the country, the RC3 supports its member organizations with awareness, education, and mentorship on a wide variety of subjects, projects, and initiatives. The RC3 is engaged in various initiatives to advance critical infrastructure security and resilience, vulnerability reduction, and consequence mitigation, including the following:

- Partnering with the Critical Infrastructure Cross-Sector Council, FSLC, and the SLTTGCC to improve information sharing and communication throughout the national partnership and identify ways the four councils can leverage each other's membership and knowledge;

- Hosting Webinars to enhance partners' understanding of the *National Plan* and its implementation;

- Conducting regional catastrophic event response and recovery exercises in conjunction with existing regional workshops;

- Identifying best practices and standards for the use of social media tools in critical infrastructure security and resilience;

- Developing a communication and collaboration strategy that embraces social media technology and employs controls and practices that are efficient, effective, and commensurate with the emerging risk environment; and

- Aiding in the development and coordination of State and local Critical Infrastructure Asset Registries.

Information Sharing and Analysis Organizations

Several private sector information sharing and analysis organizations have been established in the last decade. ISACs are examples of successful information-sharing organizations.

ISACs – ISACs serve as operational and dissemination arms for many sectors and subsectors, and facilitate sharing of information between government and the private sector. ISACs work closely with SCCs in the sectors where they are recognized. They are designed to provide in-depth sector analysis and help coordinate sector response during incidents, including information sharing within sectors, between sectors, and among public and private sector critical infrastructure stakeholders. Government agencies also may rely on ISACs for situational awareness and to enhance their ability to provide timely, actionable data to targeted entities. The primary activities of an ISAC are:

- Provide trusted communities and frameworks for critical infrastructure sectors to facilitate the sharing of timely, actionable, and reliable information for situational awareness;

- Provide in-depth comprehensive sector threat and incident analysis and enable aggregation and anonymization of data;

- Provide all-hazards threat warning and incident reporting to enhance member risk mitigation activities;

- Develop and maintain, as applicable, collaborative relationships with operations centers such as the NICC and NCCIC; and

- Participate in the planning, coordination, and conduct of exercises, as applicable.

Critical Infrastructure Partnership Advisory Council

The Critical Infrastructure Partnership Advisory Council (CIPAC)[20] was established by DHS in 2006 as a mechanism to support the sectors' interests to jointly engage in critical infrastructure discussions and to participate in a broad spectrum of activities. CIPAC forums serve an advisory role by supporting deliberations on critical infrastructure issues that are needed to arrive at a consensus position or when making formal recommendations to the Federal Government. Discussions and activities undertaken after invoking CIPAC include the following:

- Plan, coordinate, and exchange information on sector-specific or cross-sector issues;

- Advise on operational activities related to critical infrastructure security and resilience, both in steady state and during incident response;

- Contribute to the development and implementation of national policies and plans, including this *National Plan* and the SSPs; and

- Submit consensus recommendations to the Federal Government related to critical infrastructure programs, tools, and capabilities.

CIPAC-covered activities convene GCC and SCC representatives when there is a need to seek consensus on an issue. As such, CIPAC may be used at the sector, cross-sector, or working group levels, depending on the topic and deliberation purpose. Meetings, forums, and other CIPAC activities are attended by government and private sector representatives, and often include invited subject matter experts who present on a specific topic.

Information Sharing for Critical Infrastructure Security and Resilience

In addition to information disseminated by SSAs and other national partnership mechanisms, there are Federal information sharing and analysis organizations that address national issues but also serve day-to-day operational roles to support SLTT entities and work with public and private owners and operators. These include the National Infrastructure Coordinating Center (NICC), the National Cybersecurity and Communications Integration Center (NCCIC), the National Operations Center (NOC), and the National Cyber Investigative Joint Task Force (NCIJTF).

NICC and NCCIC – PPD-21 states that "There shall be two national critical infrastructure centers operated by DHS—one for physical infrastructure [NICC] and another for cyber infrastructure [NCCIC]. They shall function in an integrated manner and serve as focal points for critical infrastructure partners to obtain situational awareness and integrated, actionable information to

---

[20] Critical Infrastructure Partnership Advisory Council, http://www.dhs.gov/critical-infrastructure-partnership-advisory-council

protect the physical and cyber aspects of critical infrastructure." The NICC serves as a clearinghouse of information to receive and synthesize critical infrastructure information and provide that information back to decision makers at all levels to enable rapid, informed decisions in steady state, heightened alert, and during incident response. The NCCIC is a round-the-clock information sharing, analysis, and incident response center where government, private sector, and international partners share information and collaborate on response and mitigation activities to reduce the impact of significant incidents, enhance partners' security posture, and develop and issue alerts and warnings while creating strategic and tactical plans to combat future malicious activity. PPD-21 also requires an integrated analysis component that works in coordination with both centers to contextualize and facilitate greater understanding of the information streams flowing through the two centers.

These centers, along with the integrated analysis function, build situational awareness across critical infrastructure sectors based on partner input and provide information with greater depth, breadth, and context than the individual pieces from any single partner or sector.

NOC – The NOC is the principal operations center for DHS, consisting of a NOC Watch, Intelligence Watch and Warning, FEMA's National Watch Center and National Response Coordination Center, and the NICC. The NOC provides situational awareness and a common operating picture for the entire Federal Government and for SLTT governments as appropriate, in the event of a natural disaster, act of terrorism, or other manmade disaster. The NOC also ensures that critical terrorism and disaster-related information reaches government decision makers.

NCIJTF – The FBI is responsible for the operation of the NCIJTF, the interagency cyber center with primary responsibility for developing and sharing information related to cyber threat investigations and for coordinating and integrating associated operational activities to counter cyber threats, including threats to critical infrastructure. The NCIJTF is an alliance of peer agencies with complementary missions to protect national cyber interests. Representatives from participating Federal agencies, including DHS, and from State, local, and international law enforcement partners, have access to comprehensive views of cyber threat situations, while working together in a collaborative environment.

Collaborative Approaches across the Critical Infrastructure Community

The partnership structures described above are designed to encourage participation from across the community and allow individual owners and operators of critical infrastructure and other stakeholders across the country to participate. The structures also are intended to promote consistency of process to enable efficient collaboration between disparate parts of the critical infrastructure community. This does not imply that the sector and cross-sector partnership structure should be replicated at the regional, State, and local levels; however, its proven utility may serve as a model and bring value at various levels.

Additional regional partnerships have brought together diverse interests across State boundaries, metropolitan areas, infrastructure sectors, and operational interests to build organizations to address shared concerns. Collaborating at the regional level requires flexibility to engage other entities that play a role in critical infrastructure security and resilience such as the FBI's InfraGard chapters, Weapons of Mass Destruction (WMD) Coordinators, Field Intelligence Groups, and Joint Terrorism Task Forces (JTTFs). JTTFs are multiagency task forces designed to combine the resources, talents, skills, and knowledge of local, State, tribal, territorial, and Federal law enforcement, as well as the Intelligence Community, into a single team that detects, investigates, analyzes, responds to, and resolves terrorist threats or incidents. Suspicious activity that may be linked to terrorism should be reported immediately to the nearest JTTF for investigation and resolution. JTTFs should be considered intake centers for reports of suspicious activity that may constitute a nexus to terrorism. JTTFs share information with other regional law enforcement, critical infrastructure partners, and State and major urban area fusion centers. The Domestic Security Alliance Council[21] also collaborates with the FBI.

DHS and FBI have robust critical infrastructure protection programs that are designed to detect terrorist threats involving critical infrastructure. For example, the Nationwide Suspicious Activity Reporting Initiative (NSI) involves DHS and the FBI partnering to raise awareness through development of threat products and targeted public flyers, placards, and public and private sector messaging. These messages are tailored to the threat and designed to obtain suspicious activity reporting from the community so that those threats can be quickly forwarded to the nearest JTTF for investigation and resolution. The DHS "If You See Something, Say Something™" campaign is an example of such public messaging.

---

[21] Domestic Security Alliance Council, http://www.dsac.gov?Pages/index.aspx

State and major urban area fusion centers help owners and operators and government partners stay informed of emerging threats and vulnerabilities. State and local government representatives (e.g., emergency management, public health, and public safety officials) may have regular interaction with fusion centers for the receipt, analysis, gathering, and sharing of law enforcement and protection information among SLTT and Federal partners. Homeland Security Advisors, Protective Security Advisors, Cybersecurity Advisors, FBI WMD Coordinators, InfraGard Coordinators, and JTTF members also interface with the fusion centers.

The State component of the critical infrastructure partnership extends beyond the SLTTGCC to include State coalitions and operational partnerships and, where possible, State-level sector-specific agencies that support the provision of essential services such as energy, telecommunications, water, and transportation. These State and regional partnerships develop integrated preparedness, security, and resilience plans based on risk analysis that accounts for local and regional factors.

Local critical infrastructure partnerships often link to local Chambers of Commerce, business roundtables, or similar coalitions of private sector companies. They also include public-private partnerships, as well as community service organizations, that support preparedness, response, and recovery.

PPD-21 calls for international collaboration as part of the national unity of effort to strengthen security and resilience. To that end, Federal, private sector, and international partners work together to implement coordinated global infrastructure security measures to protect against current and future physical and cyber threats. International collaboration occurs in many areas, including sharing information, implementing existing agreements affecting critical infrastructure security and resilience, developing policies for cross-border coordination of security and resilience initiatives, addressing cross-sector and global issues such as cybersecurity, and enhancing understanding of cross-border interdependencies of critical infrastructure.

Appendix B. Roles, Responsibilities, and Capabilities of Critical Infrastructure Partners and Stakeholders

PPD-21 states, "An effective national effort to strengthen critical infrastructure security and resilience must be guided by a national plan that identifies roles and responsibilities and is informed by the expertise, experience, capabilities, and responsibilities of the SSAs, other Federal departments and agencies with critical infrastructure roles, SLTT entities, and critical infrastructure owners and operators."

This appendix includes the Federal roles and responsibilities defined in PPD-21 and described in the document *Critical Infrastructure Security and Resilience Functional Relationships*, developed by DHS's Integrated Task Force and released in June 2013.

Recognizing the resource constraints under which both public and private sector partners operate, the roles and activities described in this appendix are not intended as requirements for any partner or stakeholder group. Many of the roles and responsibilities described below represent capabilities that various partners bring to critical infrastructure security and resilience and are provided for reference to support a common awareness of the possible roles and contributions of various participants within the critical infrastructure community.

Some additional roles and responsibilities described in the 2009 NIPP remain applicable and also are included here for the Federal Government, critical infrastructure owners and operators, SLTT governments, advisory councils and committees, and academic and research organizations.

There are certain roles and capabilities that are shared across various partner groups. These are repeated below (and tailored where appropriate) for each partner to which they apply. This allows members of the critical infrastructure community to consult the section of this appendix that is most applicable to their place in the partnership and find all their potential roles and responsibilities in one place.

Secretary of Homeland Security

PPD-21 identifies the following roles and responsibilities for the Secretary of Homeland Security.

The Secretary of Homeland Security provides strategic guidance, promotes a national unity of effort, and coordinates the overall Federal effort to promote the security and resilience of the Nation's critical infrastructure. In carrying out the responsibilities of the Homeland Security Act of 2002, as amended, the Secretary of Homeland Security:

- Evaluates national capabilities, opportunities, and challenges in securing and making resilient critical infrastructure;

- Analyzes threats to, vulnerabilities of, and potential consequences from all hazards on critical infrastructure;

- Identifies security and resilience functions that are necessary for effective public-private engagement with all critical infrastructure sectors;

- Develops a national plan and metrics, in coordination with SSAs and other critical infrastructure partners;

- Integrates and coordinates Federal cross-sector security and resilience activities;

- Identifies and analyzes key interdependencies among critical infrastructure sectors; and

- Reports on the effectiveness of national efforts to strengthen the Nation's security and resilience posture for critical infrastructure.

The Secretary of Homeland Security is the principal Federal official for domestic incident management and coordinates Federal preparedness activities in alignment with PPD-8, including coordinating Federal Government responses to significant cyber or physical incidents affecting critical infrastructure (consistent with statutory authorities). The Secretary of Homeland Security coordinates with other relevant members of the Executive Branch, as appropriate, to support a single, comprehensive approach to domestic incident management so all levels of government across the Nation have the capability to work efficiently and effectively together, using a national approach to domestic incident management.

PPD-21 identifies additional roles and responsibilities for the Secretary of Homeland Security, including:

- Identify and prioritize critical infrastructure, considering physical and cyber threats, vulnerabilities, and consequences, in coordination with SSAs and other Federal departments and agencies;

- Maintain national critical infrastructure centers that provide a situational awareness capability that includes integrated, actionable information about emerging trends, imminent threats, and the status of incidents that may impact critical infrastructure;

- In coordination with SSAs and other Federal departments and agencies, provide analysis, expertise, and other technical assistance to critical infrastructure owners and operators and facilitate access to and exchange of information and intelligence necessary to strengthen the security and resilience of critical infrastructure;

- Conduct comprehensive assessments of the vulnerabilities of the Nation's critical infrastructure in coordination with the SSAs and in collaboration with SLTT entities and critical infrastructure owners and operators;

- Coordinate Federal Government responses to significant cyber or physical incidents affecting critical infrastructure consistent with statutory authorities;

- Support the Attorney General and law enforcement agencies with their responsibilities to investigate and prosecute threats to and attacks against critical infrastructure;

- Coordinate with and utilize the expertise of SSAs and other appropriate Federal departments and agencies to map geospatially, image, analyze, and sort critical infrastructure by employing commercial satellite and airborne systems, as well as existing capabilities within other departments and agencies; and

- Report annually on the status of national critical infrastructure efforts as required by statute.

Additional DHS roles and responsibilities include:

- Establish and maintain a comprehensive, multi-tiered, and dynamic information-sharing network designed to provide timely and actionable threat information, assessments, and warnings to public and private sector partners, including protecting sensitive information voluntarily provided by the private sector and facilitating the development of sector-specific and cross-sector information-sharing and analysis systems, mechanisms, and processes;

- Sponsor critical infrastructure security and resilience-related R&D, demonstration projects, and pilot programs;

- Conduct modeling and simulations with SSAs to analyze sector, cross-sector, and regional dependencies and interdependencies (including cyber dependencies), and share the results with critical infrastructure partners, as appropriate;

- Document and apply lessons learned from exercises, actual incidents, and pre-disaster mitigation efforts to critical infrastructure security and resilience activities; and

- Evaluate the need for and coordinate the security and resilience of additional critical infrastructure categories over time, as appropriate.

Sector-Specific Agencies

PPD-21 identifies the following roles and responsibilities for the SSAs.

Each critical infrastructure sector has unique characteristics, operating models, and risk profiles. The Federal SSA or co-SSA assigned to each sector has institutional knowledge and specialized expertise about its sector(s). Recognizing existing statutory or regulatory authorities of specific Federal departments and agencies, and leveraging existing sector familiarity and relationships, SSAs:

- Coordinate with DHS and other relevant Federal departments and agencies and collaborate with critical infrastructure owners and operators, where appropriate with independent regulatory agencies, and with SLTT entities, as appropriate to implement PPD-21;

- Serve as a day-to-day Federal interface for the dynamic prioritization and coordination of sector-specific activities;

- Carry out incident management responsibilities consistent with statutory authority and other appropriate policies, directives, or regulations;

- Provide, support, or facilitate technical assistance and consultations for that sector to identify vulnerabilities and help mitigate incidents, as appropriate; and

- Support the Secretary of Homeland Security's statutory reporting requirements by providing, on an annual basis, sector-specific critical infrastructure information.

The SSAs are listed in Table B-1 below.

Table B-1 – Sector-Specific Agencies and Critical Infrastructure Sectors

Sector-Specific Agency	Critical Infrastructure Sector		
Department of Agriculture[a] Department of Health and Human Services	Food and Agriculture		
Department of Defense[b]	Defense Industrial Base		
Department of Energy[c]	Energy[d]		
Department of Health and Human Services	Healthcare and Public Health		
Department of the Treasury	Financial Services		
Environmental Protection Agency	Water and Wastewater Services		
Department of Homeland Security	■ Chemical ■ Critical Manufacturing ■ Information Technology	■ Commercial Facilities ■ Dams ■ Nuclear Reactors, Materials, and Waste	■ Communications ■ Emergency Services
Department of Homeland Security, General Services Administration	Government Facilities[e]		
Department of Homeland Security, Department of Transportation	Transportation Systems		

[a] The Department of Agriculture is responsible for agriculture and food (meat, poultry, and processed egg products).

[b] The Department of Health and Human Services is responsible for food other than meat, poultry, and processed egg products.

[c] Nothing in this plan impairs or otherwise affects the authority of the Secretary of Defense over the Department of Defense (DoD), including the chain of command for military forces from the President as Ctommander in Chief, to the Secretary of Defense, to the commander of military forces, or military command and control procedures.

[d] The Energy Sector includes the production, refining, storage, and distribution of oil, gas, and electric power. The Department of Homeland Security is the SSA for commercial nuclear power facilities and for dams.

[e] The Department of Education is the SSA for the Education Facilities Subsector of the Government Facilities Sector; the Department of the Interior is the SSA for the National Monuments and Icons Subsector of the Government Facilities Sector.

Other Federal Departments and Agencies

As stated in PPD-21, Federal departments and agencies shall provide timely information to the Secretary of Homeland Security and the national critical infrastructure centers necessary to support cross-sector analysis and inform the situational awareness capability for critical infrastructure; the centers will in turn share the information back with the appropriate critical infrastructure partners.

Federal departments and agencies that are not designated as SSAs, but have unique responsibilities, functions, or expertise in a particular critical infrastructure sector (such as GCC members) assist in identifying and assessing high-consequence critical infrastructure and collaborate with relevant partners to share security and resilience-related information within the sector, as appropriate.

The following departments and agencies—some of which also serve as SSAs—have specialized or support functions related to critical infrastructure security and resilience that shall be carried out by, or along with, other Federal departments and agencies and independent regulatory agencies, as appropriate.

Department of State

The Secretary of State has direct responsibility for policies and activities to protect U.S. citizens and U.S. facilities abroad, and is the overarching lead for U.S. foreign relations, policies, and activities as well as for the advancement of U.S. interests abroad. As part of the day-to-day diplomatic activities on behalf of the U.S. Government, the Department of State (DOS) is responsible for establishing and maintaining international partnerships that are essential to critical infrastructure security and resilience. DOS, in coordination with DHS, SSAs, and other Federal departments and agencies, coordinates with foreign governments, international organizations, and the U.S. private sector through the Overseas Security Advisory Council (OSAC), to strengthen the security and resilience of critical infrastructure located outside the United States and to facilitate the overall exchange of best practices and lessons learned for promoting the security and resilience of critical infrastructure on which the Nation depends.

Department of Defense

In support of critical infrastructure security and resilience, the Department of Defense (DoD) operates, defends, and ensures the resilience of DoD-owned or contracted critical infrastructure; defends the nation from attack in all domains, including cyber; gathers foreign intelligence and determines attribution in support of national and DoD requirements; secures national security and military systems; and investigates criminal cyber activity under military jurisdiction. The National Security Agency, as part of DoD and the Intelligence Community, provides foreign intelligence support and information assurance support to DHS and other departments and agencies per Executive Order 12333.

Department of Justice

The Department of Justice (DOJ), including the Federal Bureau of Investigation (FBI), leads counterterrorism and counterintelligence investigations and related law enforcement activities across the critical infrastructure sectors. DOJ investigates, disrupts, prosecutes, and otherwise reduces foreign intelligence, terrorist, and other threats to, and actual or attempted attacks on, or sabotage of, the Nation's critical infrastructure. The FBI also conducts domestic collection, analysis, and dissemination of cyber threat information and is responsible for the operation of the National Cyber Investigative Joint Task Force (NCIJTF). The NCIJTF is a multiagency national focal point that coordinates, integrates, and shares pertinent information related to cyber threat investigations, with representatives from DHS, the Intelligence Community, and DoD, and collaborates with SSAs and other agencies as appropriate.

Department of the Interior

The Department of the Interior, in collaboration with the SSA for the Government Facilities Sector, identifies, prioritizes, and coordinates the security and resilience efforts for national monuments and icons and incorporates measures to reduce risk to these critical assets, while also promoting their use and enjoyment.

Department of Commerce

The Department of Commerce, in collaboration with DHS, the SSAs, and other relevant Federal departments and agencies, engages private sector, research, academic, and government organizations to improve security for technology and tools related to cyber-based systems and enable the timely availability of industrial products, materials, and services to meet homeland security requirements.

Intelligence Community

The Intelligence Community, led by the Director of National Intelligence, uses applicable authorities and coordination mechanisms to provide, as appropriate, intelligence assessments regarding threats to critical infrastructure and coordinate on intelligence and other sensitive or proprietary information related to critical infrastructure. In addition, it oversees information security policies, directives, standards, and guidelines for safeguarding national security systems as directed by the President, applicable law, and in accordance with that direction, carried out under the authority of the heads of agencies that operate or exercise authority over such national security systems.

General Services Administration

The General Services Administration, in consultation with DoD, DHS, and other Federal departments and agencies, as appropriate, provides or supports government-wide contracts for critical infrastructure systems and ensures that such contracts include audit rights for the security and resilience of critical infrastructure.

Nuclear Regulatory Commission

The Nuclear Regulatory Commission (NRC) regulates its licensees' protection of commercial nuclear power reactors and non-power nuclear reactors used for research, testing, and training; nuclear materials in medical, industrial, and academic settings; and facilities that fabricate nuclear fuel; and the transportation, storage, and disposal of nuclear materials and waste. The NRC collaborates, to the extent possible, with DHS, DOJ, the Department of Energy, the Environmental Protection Agency, the Department of Health and Human Services, and other Federal departments and agencies, as appropriate.

Federal Communications Commission

The Federal Communications Commission, to the extent permitted by law, exercises its authority and expertise to partner with DHS and the Department of State, as well as other Federal departments and agencies and SSAs as appropriate, to: (1) identify and prioritize communications infrastructure; (2) identify Communications Sector vulnerabilities and work with industry and other stakeholders to address those vulnerabilities; and (3) work with stakeholders, including industry, and engage foreign governments and international organizations to increase the security and resilience of critical infrastructure within the Communications Sector and facilitate the development and implementation of best practices promoting the security and resilience of critical communications infrastructure on which the Nation depends.

Federal and State Regulatory Agencies

Some sectors are regulated by Federal or State regulatory agencies that are not the designated SSA for the sector. In these cases, regulators possess unique insight into the functioning of the critical infrastructure they oversee and bring key capabilities to the critical infrastructure partnership, including:

- Facilitating the exchange of information with critical infrastructure owners and operators during incident response and recovery;

- Encouraging critical infrastructure owners and operators to participate in public-private partnerships (e.g., through regional coalitions);

- Participating in GCCs and coordinating with SSAs on critical infrastructure security and resilience initiatives; and

- Ensuring sector resilience through the policymaking and oversight process.

Critical Infrastructure Owners and Operators

Critical infrastructure owners and operators in the public and private sector develop and implement security and resilience programs for the critical infrastructure under their control, while taking into consideration the public good as well. Owners and operators take action to support risk management planning and investments in security as a necessary component of prudent business planning and operations. In today's risk environment, these activities generally include reassessing and adjusting business continuity and emergency management plans, building increased resilience and redundancy into business processes and systems, protecting facilities against physical and cyber attacks, reducing the vulnerability to natural disasters, guarding against insider threats, and increasing coordination with external organizations to avoid or minimize the impact on surrounding communities or other industry partners.

For many private sector enterprises, the level of investment in security reflects risk-versus-consequence tradeoffs that are based on two factors: (1) what is known about the risk environment, and (2) what is economically justifiable and sustainable in a competitive marketplace or within resource constraints. In the context of the first factor, the Federal Government is uniquely positioned to help inform critical infrastructure investment decisions and operational planning across the sectors. Owners and operators may look to the government and information sharing and analysis organizations like ISACs as a source of security-related best practices and for attack or natural hazard indications, warnings, and threat assessments.

In relation to the second factor, owners and operators may rely on government entities or participate in collective efforts with other owners and operators to address risks outside of their property or in situations in which the current threat exceeds an enterprise's capability to protect itself or requires an unreasonable level of additional investment to mitigate risk. In this situation, public and private sector partners at all levels collaborate to address the security and resilience of national-level critical infrastructure, provide timely warnings, and promote an environment in which critical infrastructure owners and operators can carry out their specific responsibilities.

Critical infrastructure owners and operators participate in many risk mitigation activities including cybersecurity information-sharing efforts (e.g., sector-specific cyber working groups, the Cross-Sector Cybersecurity Working Group, and the Industrial Control Systems Joint Working Group), cyber risk assessments, cybersecurity exercises, cyber incident response and recovery efforts, and cyber metrics development. The roles of specific owners and operators vary widely within and across sectors. Some sectors have statutory and regulatory frameworks that affect private sector security operations within the sector; however, most are guided by a voluntary focus on security and resilience or adherence to industry-promoted best practices.

Within this diverse landscape, critical infrastructure owners and operators may contribute to national critical infrastructure security and resilience efforts through a range of activities. These activities may include but are not limited to: performing critical infrastructure risk assessments; understanding dependencies and interdependencies; developing and coordinating emergency response plans with appropriate Federal and SLTT government authorities; establishing continuity plans and programs that facilitate the performance of lifeline functions during an incident; participating in critical infrastructure-focused training and exercise activities with public and private sector partners; and contributing technical expertise to the critical infrastructure security and resilience efforts of DHS and the SSAs.

State, Local, Tribal, and Territorial Governments and Regional Organizations

SLTT governments implement the homeland security mission, protect public safety and welfare, and ensure the provision of essential services to communities and industries within their jurisdictions. They also ensure the security and resilience of critical infrastructure under their control, as well as that owned and operated by other parties within their jurisdictions. Their efforts are critical to the effective planning and implementation of critical infrastructure security and resilience activities. Since SLTT officials are often the first on the scene of an incident, they are critical to time-sensitive, post-event critical infrastructure response and recovery activities. State, territorial, and tribal governments are also conduits for requests for Federal assistance when a threat or incident situation exceeds the capabilities of public and private sector partners at lower jurisdictional levels.

Critical infrastructure security and resilience programs form an essential component of SLTT homeland security strategies, particularly with regard to establishing funding priorities and informing security and resilience investment decisions. To facilitate effective critical infrastructure security and resilience and performance measurement, these programs should address all core elements of this *National Plan*, where appropriate, including key cross-jurisdictional security and information-sharing linkages, as well as specific critical infrastructure security and resilience activities focused on risk management. These programs play a primary role in the identification and protection of critical infrastructure regionally and locally and also support DHS and SSA efforts to identify, ensure connectivity with, and enable the security and resilience of critical infrastructure of national significance within the jurisdiction.

State and Territorial Governments

State and territorial governments establish partnerships, facilitate coordinated information sharing, and enable planning and preparedness for critical infrastructure security and resilience within their jurisdictions. They are crucial coordination hubs, bringing together prevention, protection, mitigation, response, and recovery authorities, capabilities, and resources among local jurisdictions, across sectors, and between regional entities. States and Territories receive critical infrastructure information from the Federal Government to support national and State critical infrastructure security and resilience programs. In addition, States and Territories provide information to DHS, as part of the grants process or through homeland security strategy updates, regarding State or territorial priorities, requirements, and critical infrastructure-related funding needs.

States and Territories should work with State and territorial-level sector-specific agencies to support the vision, mission, and goals of this *National Plan* within those sectors, as appropriate, and engage subject matter experts at the sector level to assist with this effort.

State and territorial programs should address all relevant aspects of critical infrastructure security and resilience, leverage support from homeland security assistance programs that apply across the homeland security mission area, and reflect priority activities in their strategies to ensure that resources are effectively allocated. Effective Statewide and regional critical infrastructure security and resilience efforts should be integrated into the overarching homeland security program framework at the State or territorial level to ensure that prevention, protection, mitigation, response, and recovery efforts are synchronized and mutually supportive.

Critical infrastructure security and resilience at the State or territorial level must cut across all sectors present within the jurisdiction and support national, State, and local priorities. The program also should explicitly address unique geographical issues, including trans-border concerns, as well as interdependencies among sectors and jurisdictions within those geographical boundaries.

Local Governments

Local governments provide critical public services and functions in conjunction with private sector owners and operators. In some sectors, local government entities, through their public works departments, own and operate critical infrastructure such as water, storm water, and electric utilities. Most disruptions or natural hazards that affect critical infrastructure begin and end as local situations. Local authorities typically shoulder the weight of initial response and recovery operations until coordinated support from other sources becomes available, regardless of who owns or operates the affected asset, system, or network. As a result, local governments are key players within the critical infrastructure partnership. They drive emergency preparedness, as well as local participation in critical infrastructure security and resilience across a variety of jurisdictional partners, including government agencies, owners and operators, and private citizens in the communities that they serve.

Specific activities for critical infrastructure security and resilience at the State, territorial, and local level may include, but are not limited to:

- Acting as a focal point for and promoting the coordination of security, resilience, and emergency response activities, preparedness programs, and resource support among relevant jurisdictions, regional organizations, private sector partners, and citizens;

- Developing a consistent approach to critical infrastructure identification, risk determination, mitigation planning, prioritized security investment, and exercising preparedness among all relevant stakeholders within their jurisdictions;

- Identifying, implementing, and monitoring a risk management approach and taking corrective actions, as appropriate;

- Participating in significant national, regional, and local awareness programs to encourage appropriate management and security of cyber systems;

- Facilitating the exchange of security information, including threat assessments and other analyses, attack indications, warnings, and advisories, within and across entities and sectors within their jurisdictions;

- Participating in the critical infrastructure partnership, including sector-specific GCCs; the State, Local, Tribal, and Territorial Government Coordinating Council (SLTTGCC); and other relevant critical infrastructure governance and planning efforts;

- Ensuring that funding priorities are addressed and that resources are allocated efficiently and effectively;

- Sharing information on infrastructure deemed significant from a national, State, regional, local, tribal, and/or territorial perspective to enable prioritized security and restoration of critical public services, facilities, utilities, and lifeline functions within the jurisdiction;

- Documenting and applying lessons learned from pre-disaster mitigation efforts, exercises, and actual incidents;

- Coordinating with partners to promote education, training, and awareness of critical infrastructure security and resilience to motivate increased participation by owners and operators;

- Providing response and security support, as appropriate, where there are gaps and where local entities lack the resources needed to address those gaps;

- Identifying and communicating to DHS the requirements for critical infrastructure-related R&D; and

- Working with State and territorial cabinet agencies to ensure that all pertinent critical infrastructure partners are represented.

Tribal Governments

Tribal government roles and capabilities regarding critical infrastructure security and resilience generally mirror those of State and local governments as detailed above. Tribal governments are responsible for the public health, welfare, and safety of tribal members, as well as the security of critical infrastructure and the continuity of essential services under their jurisdiction. Within the critical infrastructure partnership, tribal governments coordinate with Federal, State, local, and international counterparts to achieve synergy in the implementation of critical infrastructure security and resilience frameworks within their jurisdictions. This is particularly important in the context of information sharing, risk analysis and management, awareness, preparedness planning, and security and resilience program investments and initiatives.

Regional Organizations

Regional partnerships include a variety of public-private sector initiatives that cross jurisdictional and/or sector boundaries and focus on prevention, protection, mitigation, response, and recovery within a defined geographic area. Specific regional initiatives range in scope from organizations that include multiple jurisdictions and industry partners within a single State to groups that involve jurisdictions and enterprises in more than one State and across national borders. In many cases, State governments also collaborate through the adoption of interstate compacts to formalize regionally based partnerships.

Partners leading or participating in regional initiatives are encouraged to capitalize on the larger area- and sector-specific expertise and relationships to:

- Promote collaboration among partners in implementing critical infrastructure risk assessment and management activities;

- Facilitate education and awareness of critical infrastructure security and resilience efforts occurring within their geographic areas;

- Participate in regional exercise and training programs, including a focus on critical infrastructure security and resilience collaboration across jurisdictional and sector boundaries;

- Support threat-initiated and ongoing operations-based activities to enhance security and resilience, as well as to support mitigation, response, and recovery;

- Work with SLTT and international governments and the private sector, as appropriate, to evaluate regional and cross-sector critical infrastructure interdependencies, including cyber considerations;

- Conduct appropriate regional planning efforts and undertake appropriate partnership agreements to enable regional critical infrastructure security and resilience activities and enhanced response to emergencies;

- Facilitate information sharing and data collection between and among regional initiative members and external partners;

- Share information on progress and critical infrastructure security and resilience requirements with DHS, the SSAs, State and local governments, and other critical infrastructure partners, as appropriate; and

- Participate in the critical infrastructure partnership.

State and Regionally Based Boards, Commissions, Authorities, Councils, and Other Entities

An array of boards, commissions, authorities, councils, and other entities at the State, local, tribal, and regional levels perform regulatory, advisory, policy, or business oversight functions related to various aspects of critical infrastructure operations and security within and across sectors and jurisdictions. Some of these entities are established through State- or local-level executive or legislative mandates with elected, appointed, or voluntary membership. These groups include, but are not limited to, transportation authorities, public utility commissions, water and sewer boards, park commissions, housing authorities, public health agencies, and many others. These entities may serve as State-level sector-specific agencies and contribute expertise, assist with regulatory authorities, or help facilitate investment decisions related to critical infrastructure security and resilience efforts within a given jurisdiction or geographic region.

Advisory Councils

Advisory councils provide advice, recommendations, and expertise to the government (e.g., DHS, SSAs, and State or local agencies) regarding critical infrastructure security and resilience policy and activities. These entities also help enhance public-private partnerships and information sharing. They often provide an additional mechanism to engage with a pre-existing group of private sector leaders to obtain feedback on critical infrastructure security and resilience policy and programs, and to make suggestions to increase the efficiency and effectiveness of specific government programs. Examples of critical infrastructure security and resilience-related advisory councils and their associated roles include:

- **Homeland Security Advisory Council:** Provides advice and recommendations to the Secretary of Homeland Security on relevant issues; council members, appointed by the DHS Secretary, include experts from State and local governments, public safety, security and first-responder communities, academia, and the private sector.

- **Private Sector Senior Advisory Committee:** Subcommittee of HSAC that provides the council with expert advice from leaders in the private sector.

- **National Infrastructure Advisory Council:** Provides the President, through the Secretary of Homeland Security, with advice on the security of physical and cyber systems across all critical infrastructure sectors; comprises up to 30 members appointed by the President, which are selected from the private sector, academia, and State and local governments. The council was established (and amended) under Executive Orders 13231, 13286, 13385, and 13652.

- **National Security Telecommunications Advisory Committee:** Provides industry-based advice and expertise to the President on issues and problems related to implementing National Security and Emergency Preparedness communications policy; comprises up to 30 industry chief executives representing the major communications and network service providers and information technology, finance, and aerospace companies.

Academia and Research Centers

The academic and research communities play an important role in enabling national-level critical infrastructure security and resilience, including:

- Establishing Centers of Excellence (i.e., university-based partnerships or federally funded R&D centers) to provide independent analysis of critical infrastructure security and resilience issues;

- Supporting the research, development, testing, evaluation, and deployment of security and resilience technologies;

- Supporting development and implementation of concepts, architectures, and technical strategies associated with critical infrastructure security and resilience;

- Analyzing, developing, and sharing best practices related to critical infrastructure prioritization, security, and resilience efforts;

- Researching and providing innovative thinking and perspective on threats and the behavioral aspects of terrorism and criminal activity;

- Preparing or disseminating guidelines and descriptions of best practices for physical and cyber security;

- Developing and providing suitable all-hazards risk analysis and risk management courses for critical infrastructure security and resilience professionals;

- Establishing undergraduate and graduate curricula and degree programs;

- Conducting research to identify new technologies and analytical methods that can be applied by partners to support critical infrastructure security and resilience efforts;

- Participating in the review and validation of critical infrastructure security and resilience risk analysis and management approaches; and

- Engaging and serving as a resource to local communities for efforts to enhance the security and resilience of physical and cyber critical infrastructure.